Reproachfully Yours

Reproachfully Yours

by Lucile Hasley

with Foreword by Caryll Houselander

SHEED & WARD · *NEW YORK* · 1949

To my children—Susan, Janet and Danny—
in the high hope that they won't
sue me for libel when they
grow up

Contents

Foreword

W<small>HEN</small> I come to die, if I am sufficiently conscious to con
sider which things in my life I regret, and which I rejoice in,
two things will stand out definitely on the side of joy.

One, that during a time when only the most vivid reality
could make the smallest impression on me, the worst time of
the "Great War," Lucile Hasley's writing came into my life
and did make a tremendous impression. The other, that it was
my privilege to bring her writing to the notice of Frank Sheed,
a fact which I dare to hope has something to do with the
publication of this book.

My first impression has not faded. It came when bombs were
falling and everything else was falling too, everything but the
reality of God. The falling down of everything but this one
reality is going on still, with this difference, that it was so
noisy then that it deafened, and now it is silent, therefore
much more sinister, much more dangerous.

Lucile Hasley's voice . . . reaching me across the Atlantic . . .
sounded quite clearly, quite distinctly through the din, because it was in absolute contrast to it. It goes on sounding
today just as clearly, breaking the silence, and, quite wonder-
fully, it breaks that silence with laughter.

Laughter can be an ugly thing, but it can also be the love-
liest thing there is. It is lovely when it is the expression of
humble wonder and joyous love; that is what the laughter of
Faith always is, and it is the laughter of Saints which all
through the ages has restored the balance, after the clash of
swords and the falling of cities. Lucile Hasley's laughter is of
that kind.

She is very often amused, because she always sees everything in its proper perspective, herself included, and when she is amused she is amusing. Yet even when she writes most lightly, she is never superficial, and though her writing has the spontaneity of laughter, it also has the essential quality of poetry.

She would be indignant if I called her a poet, but the quality I mean is that which somehow, almost as if by magic, weds the spirit, the meaning of a phrase to the words that express it, and results necessarily in that rarer and rarer thing, good writing.

There is probably more overworked, touched-up and polished writing today than there ever has been before, and more writers so paralyzed by their own ideal of technical perfection, that they can hardly write at all, and in all this, though there is plenty of skill, there is hardly any good writing, because, exquisitely though the writers could say it, they have nothing to say, there is no compelling drive to wed their minds to their words.

But behind Lucile Hasley's writing is the vitality of an honest and eager and exploring Faith. It gives her laughter and intense realism that essential quality which makes her words come alive and go home to us, home to our minds and to our hearts, and home to stay. Such faith cannot be confined to an ivory tower in the mind, or to the limitations of a mania for self-perfection; it must radiate, it must go outwards and seize upon everything in the substantial everyday world, mixing into it, transforming it.

It is, as Christ said all Faith should be, yeast giving lightness to our lumpy dough, salt giving tang and savor to our insipid souls.

May the fundamental seriousness of this entertaining book go home to us, and when, as we shall do, we laugh out loud with the writer, may our laughter too, be like that of the Saints: restoring the balance after the clash of swords and the falling of cities.

CARYLL HOUSELANDER

Grateful acknowledgment is hereby made for the kind permission of the respective editors to reprint as follows:

THE SIGN: "Baby," "I Like Priests," "The Pigtail Stage," "Confession and Me," "To Each His Own," "I Like Married Life," "How to Make a Convert Singlehanded," "Magazine Mummie," "The Alien Corn," "The Mona Lisas," "Here We Go Round the Mulberry Bush."

EXTENSION: "Reproachfully Yours," "The First Year," "Loopholes."

WOMAN's DAY: "Hot Ball," "A Little Peach in the Orchard Grew."

MISSIONARY SERVANT: "Grandma Called It Sloth," "My Public, Right or Wrong."

THE MARIANIST: "Nightmare of an Apostle."

Reproachfully Yours

Reproachfully Yours

Born Catholics invariably say tenderly: "Ah . . . a convert. You don't know how fortunate you are, my dear. You converts have that freshness of discovery that we have missed."

Freshness of discovery. (Father, forgive them, they know not what they say.) It has never occurred to these unthinking ones that a certain "freshness of discovery" also awaits the timorous soldier sent into the thick of battle, bombs bursting in air, after only a brief basic training. And while that soldier may eventually win the status of veteran—proud, even, of his scars—one must not belittle that first shock of actual participation, the shattering repercussions.

Now that the smoke of my own battle has more or less lifted, I—like General Eisenhower—have jotted my memoirs. Let those who will, pause and reverently bend their heads with me in memoriam.

I entered the Church primed to the gills with doctrine but knowing next to nothing about church rituals. That instructor-priest of mine had completely forgotten (cleverly forgotten, I should say) to warn me that the Church has, since Pentecost, A. D. 33, lost a little of its early simplicity. I won't say that I expected to see fishermen mending their nets on the church steps, but I . . . ah, well, we all have our own little childish dreams to bury.

Today, there is a maze of ritual that makes the Changing of the Guard, Presentation at Court, or even a full-blown Coronation seem very slipshod indeed. Yet, and here is the

1

burden of my plaint, no one presented me with an equivalent
of *Robert's Rules of Order* as I timidly crept in that front
door. I was left to grapple singlehanded with a set-up that
presented all the formidable problems of an army obstacle
course. I finally ran the length of it—banging over hurdles,
crawling under the underbrush, scaling the barricades—but I
still feel, reproachfully, that someone should have warned me.

This may sound fantastic to that born Catholic who bobs
and bends and kneels as unconcernedly as if he were taking
off his galoshes, but the convert will understand. I came from
a fool's paradise that exacted nothing, and so did nothing to
toughen me up. There was no now-you-sit, now-you-kneel,
now-you-stand, now-you-dip procedure to interfere with the
deliciously dull comfort of being propped upright in a pew
and then left strictly alone.

True, it was difficult to remember that I was not attending
a P.T.A. meeting, a Democratic rally, or a town hall lecture,
but I was as comfortable as a setting hen. Weep for Adonais!
Weep, for here now is a pray-by-pray account of this raw
neophyte—jarred loose from Protestant moorings—facing the
Holy, Roman, Catholic, and Apostolic Church. . . .

I go up the church steps with the other parishioners, carefully bearing in mind that we are now united in the Mystical
Body, but nobody else seems to be thinking the same thing.
No one speaks to me. No one speaks to me from one liturgical
year to the next. There is a different turnover for each Mass,
and they all appear to remain strangers from generation
unto generation. (In the Protestant church, with one eleven
o'clock service, you know almost everyone and, if you *are* a
stranger, the minister enthusiastically pumps your hand in the
vestibule, seemingly tickled to death. In the Catholic church,
between assembly line shifts, you're lucky to get out alive and
untrampled, let alone being introduced to anyone.)

But, after awhile, I *do* begin to acquire a nodding acquaintance. That is, after seeing a certain Back go up and a certain Face return from Communion a goodly number of times,
I begin to fancy I really know the person. When one day we

meet downtown I instinctively say "Hello" and I get back a startled, uncertain echo. I find that there is an unnerving quality about a "the-face-is-familiar-but-I-haven't-the-faintest idea-who-you-are" social structure like this.

I enter the church portals—with all the confidence of a novice tightrope walker with no net underneath—and here my trials begin, sharpened by little aesthetic shocks all along the way. It is one thing to dip my hand in holy water—a very appealing sacramental—but it is quite another to dip my hand in the font and encounter a dry sponge. However, I proceed, with a fine nonchalance, to cross myself with my dry-as-toast fingertips and thus gird myself for the next hurdle: FIND A SEAT.

The back pews are disconcertingly roped off and the choice, secluded side seats are already taken. In fact, I suddenly and wildly realize that the place is packed to the rafters. The good-looking usher (how does the pastor sift the grain from the chaff—a beauty contest?) comes to my rescue, but I question his judgment as he stops and stands implacably at the most overcrowded pew. Obviously my good-looking friend is secretly hoping for a first degree miracle to rock Rome: i.e., two bodies to occupy the same space at the same time.

However, I do manage to wedge myself in, and there I am, squashed in between strangers: the man to the left wearing a wet, steamy-smelling raincoat, his arms crossed like Sitting Bull; the lady to the right fumblingly trying to untangle her knotted rosary. (The last knot comes out, victoriously, with "Ite, Missa est.")

There is just enough room to move my right arm a little, and thus I am able to poke my pocketbook and gloves behind me and so have more leeway for this business of kneeling. My tender Presbyterian knee joints protest violently against this rugged treatment, but it isn't the actual gymnastics that get me but the problem of judicious timing.

I bob up and down at all the wrong places, and I am always furtively crossing myself or administering three sharp raps on my chest after everyone else is through. It is probably this feeling of insecurity that has led me to the use of the missal, for

I figure that if I'm deeply engrossed in the printed page it won't be so noticeable if I fail to coordinate perfectly. My Mystical Body members will think, "Absent-minded, yea, but definitely holy." (It takes months to convince myself that nobody is paying the slightest attention to me.)

I am, then, on my knees, missal in hand, and all the fluttering ribbons properly adjusted. The priest enters. I flounder to my feet. His vestments may be either white, rose, green, red, purple, or black, but—they are very seldom what I'm expecting. I give one frenzied look at his color scheme and immediately begin readjusting the fluttering ribbons. I hope I'm right, what with all those tricky Collects, but who knows? Sometimes I fancy my guardian angel is breathing over my shoulder, deprecatingly shaking his head like a kibitzer.

Yet all goes smoothly to the outward eye (I hope) until suddenly I am aware that the good-looking usher has crept up on me, like the fog, on little cat feet, intent on seat money. (Fumble, fumble . . . no, that's a St. Christopher medal . . . here's a dime . . . no, no, that's a silver penny. Will the good-looking gentleman settle, I wonder, for this bus slug?)

Finally I come up with a dollar bill and receive, trustingly, the handful of change. Again I bend my head over the missal, already two pages in arrears, but it's a lost cause. Too soon, too soon, the Cat-Feet are with me again. This time it is comparatively simple—I have only to drop the regular envelope into the basket, remembering that the special coal collection envelope goes in on the *next* round—but one must be astute and alert. The few times I've had my tithe ready I've detected a fleeting look of disappointment on the handsome brow of Cat-Feet. He definitely prefers, patiently and forbearingly, to shake the basket—ever so slightly—under my nose.

Still, all this is as nothing. Anyone who has ever participated in a wedding ceremony knows that the endlessness of the aisle, the clammy hands, the constricted throat, are not mere fiction. Has it ever occurred to the calloused, cradle Catholic that a tenderfoot convert might feel the same symptoms going up to Communion? (Is this the time? If I rush up too early I'll have to make a two-point landing on my knees in the aisle, and I'd

better not tempt fate. I don't do too well without a pew to
hang onto. Yet, if I hesitate too long, I may get caught alone
—horror of horrors—at the altar rail, at the mercy of an
altar boy who may or may not turn around. No, the safe
thing is to hit the middle of the stream, protectively flanked
on all sides. But, shall I leave my pocketbook, gloves, and
missal behind or carry them along? When I come back shall
I stay at the end of the pew or climb over all those knees
again? What if I fail to find, not only the right pew, but *any*
pew to welcome me back again? Maybe I'll just have to keep
right on marching down the aisle and on out into Taylor
Street . . . ! If so, will someone follow me with a lighted
candle?)

I don't know what method other people use in order to find
their seats again, but method there must be. One day I picked
out a nearby green hat, with a flourishing flower and vegetable
garden atop, to serve as my beacon light. All would have gone
well except that my simple peasant mind hadn't considered
the possibility of the green hat going to Communion too.
This threw me completely off base.

The next Sunday I cunningly decided to count the registers
in the aisle in order to find my way home again, but I found
I bumped into too many people with my eyes glued to the
floor. ("Holy, yea, but definitely ox-like.")

But the *next* Sunday I hit it. (I really had but one choice
left outside of bringing my own monogrammed camp stool.) I
simply had to get there early enough to establish a beach-
head under a stained glass window on the side. I picked out
my window with liturgical care—it had to be not so far back
that I couldn't see the priest, nor so close to the front that
I would land with the school children—and that window has
been doing yeoman service ever since. It reads: "In memory of
the Coquillard Family" and I think of all the Coquillards,
dead and alive, with a real affection.

But one Sunday I slipped in the side door for a seven-thirty
Mass and daringly nestled down in the second row from the
front, smack in the middle. "I'm a big girl now," I reasoned.
"I'll just give this a try."

Mother Machree! I later discovered that I was firmly imbedded in the Children of Mary Sodality that eventually arose and surged forward, impressively, to receive Communion in a body. (Why didn't someone *tell* me these things?) I tried to shrink back into the very woodwork as they left me huddled there alone, a miserable focus for all eyes. ("Why is that poor little wretch remaining behind? Is she unworthy to join her sisters?")

All these perils await me in a simple half-hour Mass. I have said nothing as yet of the fancier, more intricate Sundays. There was my first Palm Sunday when I innocently arose with the rest of the congregation for the gospel, little knowing what was in store for me. It was standing thus that I caught my first true intimations of the endlessness of Eternity. I stood and stood and *stood* waiting for the signal that would, if it were not already too late, release me for a few more years of useful living.

Afterwards, they presented me with a spray of palm leaves (the Purple Heart would have been more like it) and I proudly bore them homeward. They were mine to dispose of—I had earned them, hadn't I?—and so I handed them to my two little neighbor girls who were playing in the front yard. They were merrily chasing each other with the palms, playing horse, when their born Catholic mother appeared on the scene. Let us kindly draw a veil over the ensuing tableau. Suffice it to say that my palms were returned to me (correctly braided), along with a brief homily on Catholic Culture. Catholic Culture said palms, correctly braided, were to be stuck behind a holy picture. (Question: How does one, according to Catholic Culture, eventually dispose of ancient, brittle, but obviously holy and correctly braided palm leaves?)

Are you beginning to see what I mean? I shall never, never, never get caught up with this Catholic Church. I get the use of the missal down cold—well, medium cold—and then a zealous soul presents me with the Office of Prime, Office of Compline, and an Ordo bristling with things called Simple (ha!), Semi-Double, Greater Double, Double of the Second Class. (If you, dear reader, don't know what I'm talking about, I feel better already.)

And all the extra-curricular activities! Novenas, Stations of the Cross, First Fridays, Exposition, the Rosary, Forty Hours, Retreats, Holy Hours, Communion Breakfasts, Sodalities, May Processions, Triduums . . . and—down the line—Benefit Bridges, Turkey Raffles, Church Carnivals, Rummage Sales, Bingo, the Bengal Bouts. . . .

Oh, happy, happy Protestant days when life was a song, and I had nothing more to haunt me than an annual Chicken Pie Supper in the Primary room! I laughed scornfully when I read, in a recent best seller: "They (Catholics) don't read certain books, they eat fish on Friday, and in a magic way become heirs to the life eternal. In one form or another, we all seek refuge in some such dream."

Ho! Let that gay, blithe author but enter the fold and see for herself how simple, how dream-like it all is. Believe me, the Church's theme song is not:

Row, row, row your boat gently down the stream . . .
Merrily, merrily, merrily, merrily, life is but a dream.
My interpretation would go somewhat like this:
Pull, pull, pull your oars, as hård as you can bear . . .
Warily, warily, warily, warily, life is but a snare. . . .

Do I sound as if my cup were filled to the bitter brim? Are you terribly sorry for me? Good. All I wanted was to play on the heartstrings of you reared-from-the-cradle Catholics and let you share with me my "freshness of discovery." Remember, chums?

And now quit sniffling. I'm all right, honest I am. My Catholic tribulations have only served to unite me in a closer bond, spiritually, with the early martyrs of the Church and they have in no way impaired my physical well-being. If anything, these Catholic maneuvers are grooming me for . . . well, it's anyone's guess, of course, and the possibilities are intriguing . . . but I just *might*, under the tutelage of Mother Church, surprise everyone by developing a strong character some day.

In the long interim, I would like to put in a word for my fellow converts: that mighty army of raw, untested recruits for the Church Militant. Pierced as my heart is with compassion in their behalf, I would end my saga with a fine im-passioned plea for a little sympathy to be mixed with the congratulations next time you bump into a convert.

To begin with, would you mind, terribly, burying that trite bromide about our knowing more about the religion than you do? That's mental cruelty. We're still in kindergarten and we know it. And would you mind burying at the same time that old chestnut, that embarrassing cliché, that goes: "Well, you know what they say. It's the convert that makes the best Catholic every time."

Look, while we're about it, why not have a jolly little funeral? You get busy with this spade and bury all those proverbs about converts, and I'll find some nice liturgical prayers for the dead. That is, I'll find some if luck is with me. Hmmmmm . . . let's see . . . I had it just a minute ago . . . went something like "Out of the depths" . . . here, what's this? . . . *Prayers over the Catafalque* . . . hmmmmm . . . what's a catafalque?

Oh, fiddle . . . here, you find it. Give me the spade.

Baby

I RAN across the ad one bright Sunday morning in October. I'd been looking through the TRIBUNE'S classified section for a spinet piano when this ad leaped out at me in all its desperate urgency:

"Leaving town. Must sacrifice immediately my beautiful antique rosewood square piano. 1612 Fairview Avenue."

Antique! I draw a circle around the ad, feeling that familiar warm excitement of the chase. I wasn't positive just what a square piano looked like—maybe like a harpsichord?—but as I hustled out to Fairview I began to fall in love with just the sound of it. Antique rosewood. A little antique rosewood square.

One good look at that rosewood job and my love died a-borning. I mumbled something to the effect that I wouldn't be able to handle it—that I lived in a house, not a stadium —but the Fairview woman grabbed at my arm. (Right from the beginning, she seemed to like me.) She asked me, in all fairness, just to stand and get used to the scale of it. She said—O blessed fantasy!—that it would grow on me.

So, to humor the woman, I stood and stared at her piano. I would no more have installed that thing in my living room than I would have installed a threshing machine. And yet . . . and yet . . .

Once you were adjusted to that nine-foot wingspread and Chestertonian girth, the piano's waxed and glowing beauty began to creep over you. It was like gazing at the majestic

grandeur of Fujiyama. There was inlaid mother-of-pearl over
the keyboard, and the keys themselves, of a pale yellow ivory,
were in perfect condition. The elephantine carved legs shone
as softly as old silver. *And* it was around a hundred years old.
I heard myself, as if under the influence of ether, asking the
price.

"Only one hundred dollars, a sacrifice," said the Fairview
woman, and her face began to pucker. She had, she said, taken
care of that piano like a baby. She began, between sniffles, to
give me the baby's formula: rub well with linseed oil and
paste wax, cover in damp weather, never let the furnace go
out . . .

Her grief troubled me. Surely the least I could do was to
take the piano, all two hundred cubic feet of it, and adopt
it as my own. But was I prepared for motherhood? Carefully,
I weighed the pros and cons. If *I* adopted it, the piano's
classical days were clearly over. All *I* could play, straight
through, was "A Kiss in the Dark." On the other hand, I
could promise it an oil-heated, decent, Christian home, and I
felt reasonably sure my husband would grow to love it too.

But my sentimentality didn't blunt my native shrewdness.
I didn't intend to turn the sword in that woman's heart by
flailing out "A Kiss in the Dark" on those lovely keys, but
neither did I intend to buy a pig in a poke.

I asked *her* to play something. She sat down, rippled off a
few bars of Debussy (it sounded good), and then dissolved into
tears. This was all I needed to clinch the deal. If she was *this*
attached to the piano, it must be a gem. Glory, she might
even change her mind about parting with it. I hastily wrote
out the check and, patting the woman's hand, promised to
keep her late piano warm and happy.

I felt wonderful. Consider the sheer size of my bargain.
Up to now I had brought home—in the way of antiques—
nothing bigger than some hand-painted china eggcups.

But when the piano arrived (the firm of Wallace and Black
had wisely dispatched their four beefiest pluguglies) even I
was startled afresh. My husband just stood there, leaning
weakly against the porch railing. The piano legs were dis-

membered and wrapped in old brown flannel, and the torso was covered with a dirty green canvas.

The movers set it down on the ground between the sidewalk and the curbing and then sat down on the truck's running board to rest. The neighbors, like vultures, started gathering around it as if it were a huge whale washed up on shore. How—if I *really* wanted it—was that Moby Dick ever to get through our front door? One sidewalk engineer suggested just setting it up in the front yard and building a sort of Chinese pagoda round it.

But my four beefy friends, although still panting and sweating profusely, knew what they were about. They arose from the running board—stimulated by their audience—and removed the front door from its hinges and strengthened the porch steps with planks. Then with many a grunt and shout of "Hike!" they tilted the piano sidewise, walked the planks, and heaved it into my living room. Only a very little white paint was scraped off the doorway.

Now, a square piano is nothing to have even strong men push all over your house in order to see where it looks best. Something told me that I could not order these human gorillas around as I did my own husband—i.e., walk around with a piano while I stood in one spot, my lips thoughtfully pursed.

My husband—covering up his fright with hysterical jesting—wanted it left squarely in the middle of the living room where our daily life could revolve round it. It could be used, with the top down, for pool or ping-pong or Sunday night buffet suppers. (He was really so frightened that I forgave his obvious straining to be funny. The piano would grow on him.)

We finally placed my musical bargain under the stairway, where it stuck out only about six inches. After a few days we got used to mashing our hipbones on it as we rounded the corner, and life settled down to smaller worries.

Namely, dusting. To dust my piano I had to put on my slacks and tennis shoes and carefully climb up on the top of it. I could have used the long-handled floor mop, but what would that Fairview woman have thought? Besides, I had to

put on the slacks anyway to crawl under the piano and reach
the fourth carved leg in the corner.

You would be surprised, though, how well a piano of that
size snuggled into our small living room. We didn't even have
to take out the davenport. Just two chairs and a bookcase.
The only real drawback was that the remaining furniture,
under the shadow of Fujiyama, seemed to sort of shrivel;
look like doll furniture for a family of Lilliputians.

But there was no denying that my pianoforte, itself, was
impressive, even though it did cry aloud for a Jose Iturbi to
go with it. To make up for no Iturbi, I bought an *Etude* and
spread it open, for effect, to the page that looked hardest. Lots
of little grace notes. Then I set some crystal hurricane lamps
on the shining rosewood top, and there you were. Beauty.
Antiquity. Culture.

Only it was odd the way it struck others. The more worldly
ones thought it needed a permanent torch singer perched on
top, twisting a red chiffon handkerchief and singing "My
Man." The more somber ones thought it looked like Grant's
tomb and wanted to buy me a wax funeral wreath. The ones
that mashed their hipbones on it were even more vivid in
their reactions.

But the name that finally stuck was just—Baby. It was my
Baby, said they, formula and all, and I was stuck with it. All
this I took in good spirits, but when someone would start
running a knowing hand over the keyboard I would stop him.

Well, *naturally,* I said, the thing was out of tune. You
wouldn't expect to haul a piano clear across town without
jarring it. *Naturally* my piano was a little off key (it really
set your teeth on edge), but the piano tuner was coming.

I shall always be grateful that no one was around when
that piano tuner showed up. He walked in, glanced at Baby,
winced, and then advanced grimly. He ran a scale and then
turned to me as I hung over the piano, fatuously waiting for
his congratulations.

"Buy this from a lady out on Fairview?" he asked.

I nodded. "She's living in Akron, Ohio, now," I said. I could
still see her tear-filled eyes.

"Yep," he said, "it's the same one. Tried to tune it once and I wouldn't touch it again for anything. She found it in a farmer's barn in Michigan and polished it up."

"But it's a beautiful thing," I cried. "I'll bet they used to build pianos lots better than they do now and this is around one hundred years old."

He was already sidling toward the door. "Lady," he said, "a Stradivarius improves with age, not a piano. The life span of the ordinary piano is forty years. A hard-used studio piano gives out in about ten. *This* is a wreck. It's worth about a nickel."

According to his figures, I was out exactly $99.95. Indignantly, I called another tuner and this medicine man, to my delight, briskly opened his little satchel. He said he *liked* old squares. But it unnerved me to see him applying splints and tourniquets to the brittle bamboo hammers with just plain string and glue.

As he struck the notes he kept blowing on a little silver tuning fork. Finally he said, "It's still about an octave too low. You couldn't accompany a clarinet on it. Do you mind?"

No, drat it, I didn't want any traffic with a clarinet. I only wanted my own sweet hunk of piano for myself. So he took his departure (and $8.00) and I sat down and played "A Kiss in the Dark." Soft, mellow, low.

In a few days, it was even lower. Middle C was something out of this world but I soon learned, with a little adroitness, to play around it. Yet, while it was true that Baby's Middle C was the touchiest of the keys, do not think the other keys remained aloof in robust health. With an admirable *esprit de corps* they had all, at the end of a week, slipped quietly away together into the bass section.

Back came the tuner. "Ah," he said with a fond little chuckle, "these old boys need a delicate hand, a little coaxing," and out came the string, glue, tweezers, and silver pipe. That time, for an old and probably permanent customer, he only charged $5.00.

That was only the beginning. Baby was *always* ailing, and I began to understand the brooding maternity of the Fairview woman. In time, even the tuner became so attached to Baby that I think he would have considered night calls.

Finally my husband took over. Unable to get hospitalization for Baby, my husband declared he was unable to support the tuner any longer. One afternoon he carefully watched the man, as he sat blissfully playing with the string and glue and daintily plucking out bits of moth-eaten felt with the tweezers, and decided he had it down cold.

For a while my husband's new job (certainly more fascinating than teaching American Lit. at Notre Dame) interested him mightily. He went around saying anyone could tune a piano. True. Anyone *could* tune Baby, but no one on God's green earth could keep him that way.

It got so that I would meet my husband at the door evenings and silently hand him the string and glue. Maybe *other* wives handed their tired husbands the evening newspaper and their comfy bedroom slippers, but not me. Just string and glue.

Then it happened. One day I came home from a shopping tour (I'd run down the *cutest* antique corn meal grinder) and found my husband rocking contentedly on the front porch. He hadn't looked so happy and carefree for weeks. He had that swallowed-the-canary look on his face; you could almost see the feathers sticking out of his mouth. When I asked what was up, he just kept on rocking and smiling.

I marched suspiciously into the house and then stopped cold in my tracks. My well-nigh empty living room echoed with my stricken cries of bereavement. Baby was gone.

Baby, it turned out, was now living in the basement of the First Baptist Church. They needed a piano and, as my husband pointed out, their Friendly Workshop was just the organization to keep Baby in trim. He also pointed out (with the deadly logic of husbands when goaded) that since I had adopted Baby without his permission, it was his privilege to deposit Baby on someone else's front steps. Marriage, said my husband, was give and take.

I often think about Baby in the long lonely evenings (Is he warm? Is he happy as a Baptist?) and also about that woman living in Akron, Ohio. I know just how lost she must feel.

I Like Priests

Priests are just about my favorite people. I offer this little nosegay in all simplicity: no axe to grind, no wood to chop, no bin to fill. (My child hasn't just broken a church window nor my husband been kicked out of the Holy Name Society.) I just *like* priests as people—it's as simple as that— and it doesn't hurt anything, does it, to toss a very human tribute in their direction?

They get plenty of the other: formal testimonial banquets, gala jubilee celebrations, a general bowing and scraping just because they're priests. I won't go into that side of it (although I'm just as impressed with Holy Orders, *per se*, as the next person) because respect-for-the-cloth is well taken care of. And I, too, hail all the heroic chaplains, blood-spilling missionaries, and—in particular—the priests who plug away at unpopular causes. Only I'm not hailing them here.

All I'm offering here is my little nosegay (home-grown, hand-plucked) to priests in general, along with an explanation as to just why, for Pete's sake, I enjoy them so much. To tell you the truth, it has rather puzzled me. I haven't been exactly brooding about it, understand, but I had to figure the reasons out for my own satisfaction.

Heaven only knows that priests can, in their struggle to keep you on the straight and narrow, cause you plenty of trouble; you might just as well try to budge Boulder Dam as get a priest to back down on even one teeny little doctrinal point. I've tried. Too, these priests can badger the daylights out of you trying to work off a parish debt: push you around,

hound you into doing all sorts of things you don't want to do.
They have a way of sticking out that shepherd's crook and
grabbing you around the neck before you know what's happening.

To like them in spite of all this really calls for a sound,
scholarly, and masterful explanation.

To begin with, let me say that I live in a town that not
only sports a Catholic spire every few blocks but also flaunts
nearby the golden dome of Notre Dame. The place fairly
swarms with priests and so this isn't a case of having met up
with, and been dazzled by, a lone Bing Crosby number, some
wandering clerical minstrel. I've met lots of priests (including
many that M-G-M wouldn't even screen-test for a B picture)
and I think—say I, judiciously stroking my chin—that I've
met a fair cross-section. It isn't likely that I, like a magnet,
have drawn only the fairest, the finest, the bonniest of the
lot, for things like that just don't happen to me. I'm more
the type that works like a magnet in reverse.

Peering through my microscope, then, at this cross-section, I
must first report that there are more different *kinds* of priests
than you can shake a stick at. I don't mean different orders;
I mean different species within an order. It is only recently
that I discovered this and the discovery pleases me enormously.

I'd always thought of the Roman collar as a sort of in-
delible trademark that guaranteed a uniform product: little
tin soldiers, straight off the assembly line, with the same
regulation thoughts, regulation attitudes, regulation stomach
ulcers. Not so. They've all got the same Captain, they're
all fighting under the same banner, but the Light Brigade
charges forward with a different horse for every rider.

Some priests are all wrapped up in the liturgy. (They're
the type you greet over the phone with "A happy St. Poly-
carp's feast day to you, Father.") Others are all engrossed in
the lay apostolate. ("This is Apostle #35679 reporting,
Father.") Others are working like mad to spread this or that
devotional practice. ("But I made the First Fridays, Father. I
got a Happy Death all sewed up. What's next?") Others are
struggling against odds for racial justice. ("Only Blessed Mar-

tin would get me out on a night like this, Father. I wouldn't do it for a white man.") Still others concentrate on making converts. ("I got a prospect for you, Father. If you can comfort her as to why unbaptized babies can't go to heaven, she's ours.")

Some priests live in ivory towers; some in the marketplace; some in the classroom; some in editorial offices; some on the golf courses. Some are heaven-bent on winning new souls; others in preserving and polishing the souls already won.

It's wonderful. Just pick your horse, pick your gait (plod, trot, or gallop), and stay on the highway.

All of which leads up to why I, personally, like priests as people. Because of their diversity and because of their very *business*, they never bore me. (Note: this sweeping statement applies only to priests when "off duty." It does not necessarily apply to pulpit performances!) In talking with them, I never find myself swallowing a yawn or gazing furtively at my wrist-watch or mentally planning the menu for supper. I wish I could say the same for all my acquaintances.

This priestly business deals with human nature—not haberdashery, nor wholesale groceries, nor weather stripping—and so it has a universal appeal. I don't have to listen to the one-sided interests of the small business man, the fearful moanings about inflation, nor any of that "So I up and sez to the boss" stuff. I have to listen to other things—yes—but a good rousing tirade against adultery, for instance, is more interesting than a gnashing-of-teeth at the government. The saints are more interesting than strike leaders; the benefits of the sacraments more absorbing than the benefits of weather stripping.

But although this heaven business is mighty interesting, my nosegay is for the priests themselves, not their business. That needs no floral offering. I'm presenting my posies to the priests because they don't suffer from cheerophobia. (I'm pretty proud of that word. It means "fear of having fun.") Four out of five—by actual smoke test—have a certain joyousness that you find in no other walk of life. I don't see why this light-heartedness should go along with poverty, chastity, and obedience (a combination that *I* wouldn't have dreamed up for a joyful life) but it seems to.

Maybe we, the laymen, are somewhat responsible? Maybe the laughs we hand them offset the headaches? Anyway, this business of theirs—dealing with us poor devils and our half-baked ideas—appears to give priests a shining little virtue that isn't listed among the cardinal virtues but should be. A very live and wiggling sense of humor. The sacraments, in themselves, are pretty overwhelming but sacraments pertain to people and the minute *we* enter the picture, in creeps the ridiculous . . . all mixed up with the supernatural. For example, the Sacrament of Penance.

"How in the world," say I to the hospital chaplain, "do you manage confessions in a ward? It's bad enough looking you right in the eyes in a private room let alone having an audience."

"Oh, that?" says he. "Nothing to it." And he pulls a big hunk of cotton wadding out of his coat pocket. "I just go around and plug up their ears. The Protestants all grin and tell me not to bother, that they really don't mind listening, but I plug them up anyway."

See what I mean? A wonderful sacrament, but you can't help chortling (or at least I can't) at the picture of the bed-ridden: their eyes bulging with curiosity, their frustrated ears bulging with cotton.

Fencing with the odd quirks of human nature day after day and having the smelly, boring little sins of humanity dumped on them Saturday after Saturday, a priest—I maintain—has to develop a sense of humor or else go crazy. Few go crazy.

Yet few parishioners suspect this (I mean, not that their priests aren't crazy but that they have this subterranean humor) for the average parishioner has only a nodding acquaintance with his parish shepherd. It's reduced to a "Good morning, Father" (brief tug at the hat brim) and the "Bless me, Father, for I have sinned" in the dark anonymity of the confessional. It's really too bad, but you can't exactly blame the layman. It's his loss but not his fault.

There's your priest: moving majestically from the Epistle

side to the Gospel side and then facing, solemnly, his flock.
There's a long-winded letter from the Bishop to be read; a
listing of all the sodality meetings to be held that week; and a
rather distressing financial report. (Into each life some rain
must fall. The new window shades for the school cost—woe!
woe!—a little more than the income netted from the Turkey
Raffle.) The whole discourse is lavishly sprinkled with the regulation phrases: "Hearty co-operation . . . indeed most edifying . . . wish to commend the excellent chairlady . . . we most
earnestly urge. . . ."

Is this the whole man? God forbid. But I "most earnestly
urge" you to invite him over to dinner some evening and find
out for yourself. Not only will it be "indeed most edifying"
for you (he's intelligent, he's funny, he's down to earth) but
it's good for the priest. It's good for him to see how the other
half, the seamier side, lives. It will also give him a deeper
insight as to just why mother finds it a wee bit difficult to
conduct a family rosary after supper. So by all means have
the kids milling around; don't farm them out to the neighbors
in order to present a smooth and quiet home front. Then,
after a good rousing family session, your priest will go back
to the quiet of his rectory with a new joy and contentment in
his vocation. Everybody happy.

Some of the Notre Dame priests have a razor-edge wit and
a sparkling repertoire of stories that practically comes under
the heading of professional entertainment. (And it's *good*. It's
easily worth serving up that eight dollar ham and your last
jar of prize watermelon preserves.) On a more amateur basis,
however, let me introduce Father X, a young assistant parish
priest.

Casual and ambling in his gait, he is referred to as the
Reverend Stepin Fetchit. Slow, yes, but that he does step and
that he does fetch are testified to by his army of converts, for
this is his specialty: drawing both heathens and Catholic
fallen-aways over the line. His method is fairly primitive. He
just slouches there in a chair and lets you do all the talking,
giving you enough rope to hang yourself. Then he unslouches
and unties the noose.

But it's in the confessional that he really shines like a phosphorescent cross in the dark. He appears to have (I must wring this out of him someday) some sort of a mystical X-ray machine on his side of the sliding door. The plates are quickly developed there in the dark room—clearly showing up the mote in your eye, the thorn in your flesh—and these impediments he removes with a neat surgical dispatch that would put the Mayo Brothers to shame. And for free! You go to a doctor and start out, "Doc, I got a funny little pain" and you pay plenty for wondering about that funny little pain. But a priest! You can have your soul turned inside out and thoroughly aired and diagnosed for absolutely nothing. It appeals to the Scotch in me.

Father's main cross (next to the parishioner who calls at 11 P. M. Saturday to ask the Sunday Mass schedule) is the penitent with only one cylinder working. This is the penitent who made his last confession seven years ago and has been merrily battering the commandments to bits ever since. Down the list he goes—with everything short of murder on the docket—and with Father X winding up wearily: "And ate meat on Friday, I suppose?"

The penitent is horrified. "Oh, *no,* Father! I wouldn't do *that,* Father!" The grossness, the crassness, the *presumption* of Father for even suggesting such a thing. The penitent is crucified.

It's like the Catholicity of the gangster with a .44 in one hip pocket and a seed pearl rosary in the other. "A queer kind of faith," ponders Father X, "but they've got *something,* haven't they? It's better than nothing, isn't it?" (N. B. With this kind of penitent Father X is the good shepherd, holding up the barbed wire for the black sheep to crawl under. But with the white sheep browsing in green pastures, he's a regular chain-gang overseer. You don't even dare *peek* over the fence into that greener, lusher pasture.)

Father X is a four-star priest but—no cheerophobia!

We drive him home from a Catholic Action meeting. "The Jehovah Witnesses," he remarks, "predict the day when the South Bend streets will be littered with the bodies of Catholic priests." And then, in fine indignation as he peers through the windshield: "And just look at the messy condition of these streets, would you!"

The Sunday parish bulletin comes out, on Pentecost, dated Septuagesima Sunday. The rectory phone starts ringing, the complaints come rolling in, the parish is—liturgically—all in a dither.

Father X is highly pleased. "I just wanted to test them out, see if any of them ever read the bulletin," he explains, airily.

For a slow moving man with a generally cautious approach to life, Father sometimes has strange fey-like impulses that amaze me. A lady parishioner, rushing madly around the corner of the church, collides with him. "A very special spring blessing on you, my dear," he pontificates and deeply carves the sign of the cross in the spring air. Her discomfiture tickles him. She doesn't know if he's kidding or if this is a bona fide blessing that requires a sinking to the knees right there on the flagstone walk.

Father is standing in the church vestibule, head bent devoutly over his Breviary. A young Academy girl rushes in, ten minutes late for Mass. "Good morning, pagan," he says courteously, without raising his head or flicking an eyelid.

Father X tiptoes into the church of a Saturday afternoon and quietly taps the shoulder of the last lady standing in the confessional line. "What's the line for," he whispers, "nylons or Kleenex?" (The Catholic corn grows tall and verdant and, as for me, my sensibilities are just sufficiently blunted to love it.)

In a special bracketing come the editor-priests. I shall probably never meet Father Ambrose or Father Hyacinth or Father Whos-sis but the mail correspondence friendships are indeed a pleasure. They start out stiffly, with the editor signing off with a "Yours in Christ." A few more encounters and he's winding up with a "Now, look, get a wiggle on with that story, will you?" and you're winding up with a "The baby's got the chicken pox—say a prayer for him, will you?"

In the editorial field, I have met but one priest who has caused me any pain. Once I wrote an innocuous little story

about a ten year old girl (Little Iodine, let us call her) at
Camp Jolly-Time. The story came out not only with a manu-
factured moral tacked on at the end but with all contrac-
tions ironed flat.

"I do not know," cried Little Iodine, instead of a good
American "I don't know." That dialogue had all the sprightly
charm of our local telephone directory. Also, Little Iodine
emerged more decently garbed than I had deemed necessary.
Instead of slipping into her tennis shorts, Iodine slipped into
a tennis *dress*. That editor made me feel as if I had tried to
palm off a sizzling opus that would never get by the U.S. mails.
(I wanted to carry this case to the Supreme Court but my husband said "No.")

The real sore spot for me, however, is that an accepted
manuscript calls for "biographical data" about the author. I
gaze with chartreuse envy at that lucky author who can start
out: "Born on a river barge on the Ganges, I grew up alone,
untamed, unlettered." Or, "I wrote the outline for this story
on the back of a soap wrapper in a concentration camp. After
three years as prisoner (during which time they never discovered my name was really Countess Amerila Von Steuppen-
guard), I finally escaped to Lapland. . . ."

Who, I wonder, is going to be entranced with my biographical data? I start out, in forthright, deadly fashion: "I have
spent my entire life in South Bend. At the age of six I broke
my leg while roller skating. In High School I made the second
string volley ball team and . . ." No, no, I can't go on. It's so
dull that I'm tempted to toss in a couple of divorces and il-
legitimate children and just *show* the Fathers Ambrose, Hyacinth, and Whos-sis what an interesting contributor they've
snared.

I lack the stamina to do this (and my husband says "No")
but one day . . . well, one day I did jazz up that autobiography
just a wee bit. Was it entrancing? All I know is that back
came a check for $2.50, paying me for my *letter* at two cents
a word. At first I was pretty impressed with myself. Did Hem-
ingway, Dos Passos, Evelyn Waugh, etcetera, get paid for their

business letters? No. But Mrs. Hasley of South Bend . . . hmmm, not bad, not bad at all.

Then I began to think it over. Was that priest intimating, by any chance, that my biographical data was just a nice bit of fiction? Well, I netted $2.50 from that priest's sense of humor but it left me rather subdued. My biographical data, these days, is written straight. Breaking my leg at the age of six is still its highlight. (Moral: It isn't easy to fool priests. Enjoy their lack of cheerophobia, if you will, but don't let it fool *you*. Our good shepherds know their business, they know their sheep.)

In conclusion, may I point out a grave omission on the part of us sheep? We have a national Be Kind to Dumb Animals Week, Better Babies Week, Better Books Week, etcetera, but positively no time set apart for our priests. I'm not exactly suggesting a Better Priests Week (the wording is not too happy) but we do need something. How can our priests possibly guess (from staring down into our impassive faces, Sunday after Sunday) just what we really think of them? The least we can do is occasionally hand them little nosegays—judiciously spaced, of course, so as not to wreak havoc with their humility —and let them know they're not wasting their fragrance on the desert air. Let them know that behind our blank Sunday faces, our inarticulate bleating of "Yes, Father," and "No, Father," there's real personal pleasure in knowing them.

Hot Ball

Iτ was Susan's first day at kindergarten, and I stood there
on the front porch smiling and waving her on as proudly as
if I were launching a transatlantic luxury liner. Let the Benjamin Franklin School carry on from here, thought I, as I
watched Susie become a small spot on the horizon.

I remember going back into the house that day and sinking
down on the davenport with the complacent feeling of "I
have done my best; the angels can do no more." For five years
I had slavishly followed all the child-rearing suggestions of
Angelo Patri, and while I don't say that I expected Susan to
shatter all records at the Benjamin Franklin, I most certainly
thought . . . well, this is a free country, isn't it? A person can
dream, can't he?

My favorite dream was that young Susan would inherit from
each of her parents only their special talents and—oh, wealth
to draw upon—my husband is an English professor who writes
poetry, while I used to teach handcraft at Camp Tannadoo-
nah. What, then, was to prevent Susan from being both poetic
and artistic? What, indeed?

The first week I greeted her daily with, "And what did you
do today, honey?" and the daily answer was "Hot Ball." That
and no more. Let me explain to the puzzled sport fan that
this is a game with a ball and if you touch the ball before it
quits rolling it "burns" you. I am proud to explain the in-
tricacies of this game for it is absolutely all I gleaned from my
child as to what went on at school. As far as I could figure out,

24

the Public School System was only interested in training future Olympic hot ball stars.

I finally gave up trying to get anything more out of her and explained to Mrs. Newcomb, who lives two doors away, that Susan was just a sensitive and reticent child, hoarding her golden new experiences. It sounded pretty good but, still, it was rather unnerving to have Mrs. Newcomb report that her Darlene was learning just *more* things. She, Darlene, had learned the Pledge of Allegiance in three days flat, and could sing, with motions, the cutest little song about "I give my right foot a shake, shake, shake." (Just why anyone should name a child Darlene, I don't know, but maybe I'm prejudiced. I just can't warm up to the child even though I have to admit she's smart. Too smart.)

Well, a month or so slipped by and then, one fine day, I saw Susan and Darlene coming down the sidewalk, triumphantly waving the first report cards of the season. I promptly waylaid them.

"Did you get a nice one?" I asked guilelessly of Darlene, and then—eagerly and unscrupulously—I read her report before she could open her mouth. It read, in a round library hand, "Darlene is intelligent beyond her years and responds beautifully. Her physical coordination is excellent. Her pleasant disposition is winning her many friends."

Then I opened Susan's. It read, in a plain unvarnished statement, "Susan appears to enjoy her contacts with the other children." No comment, you understand, as to how the teacher was enjoying *her* contact with Susan. And then there was a P. S.: "I would like to talk with you at your convenience."

With my first intimations that all was not well, I went to see the teacher. She was young, pretty, and had a firm grip on her educational principles. At the beginning of the conference I, too, had a firm grip—in fact, I was all that a pleasantly intelligent young matron should be—but as the horrible facts began to sink in, my veneer began to crack. Was this my child, my own first-born, whom she was talking about?

Susan, said she, was the most backward child in the whole room. She didn't mean to imply that she was a moron, but, well, "backward" seemed the best way to describe her. Since she had entered school she had not answered one question correctly. She either said, "Huh? What? I don't know," or else gave a 100 per cent wrong answer. She could not even learn to recognize "Jingle Bells" on the piano; she remembered absolutely nothing of stories read during the story hour. For instance, just yesterday they had had "Jack and the Bean Stalk." Today, Susan's version had gone something like this: "Jack took the beans and went down to the hotel and planted them in the lobby. They grew into a big plant and he climbed up and picked the beans and ground them into coffee." Conceivably, said the teacher, straining her charity, she had associated the castle with a hotel but, aside from that, there was certainly no connection.

I stood there like a stricken mute. "Wait," said the teacher, in a kinder tone, "I'll show you what I mean." She called Susan over and, half-kneeling, she asked in a loud, distinct voice: "Susan, what was the little girl's name in 'The Three Bears'?"

Susan looked up, her little round face absolutely void of any spark of human intelligence, and muttered, "Huh? What? I don't know."

"Susan!" I pleaded. "You *do* know what it is. Tell me."

There was only a shake of her head.

"Why, she has been telling her little sister these stories for two years," I cried out, stung to the quick; "she knows them as well as I do. She *loves* stories and her favorite is 'Alice in Wonderland,' which is certainly harder than these hinky-dinky stories. And she has a little book of nursery songs that I play on the piano and she knows them all. Why, this is ridiculous. . . ."

The teacher listened politely until I was through. "My one suggestion," said she, rather flatly, "is that she's possibly hard of hearing. You'd better have a doctor check it before we decide what to do next."

I walked out of the B. Franklin feeling terrible. I'd take her to a doctor, of course, but what did I want him to find? Did I prefer Susan to be losing her hearing or sprouting into a nice little moron? I glanced down at Susan swinging happily along at my side.

"Susan," I said, speaking at once loud and distinctly as the teacher had done, "what really was that little girl's name in the story?"

She looked surprised. "Why, you know, Mama. Goldilocks."

This time I looked at her hard. What in the world ailed the child? With my own eyes I had seen her look and act like a by-product of the Jukes family not ten minutes ago. Now I tried to look at her impersonally and coldly. Was there perhaps a vacuous look in her eyes, did her mouth perhaps gape just a trifle? I certainly couldn't see it myself, but maybe, I concluded grimly, the medical profession—not blinded by Mother Love—would.

So the next day I called the doctor on the phone and explained everything so that nothing would have to be said before Susan. It was a new doctor for us, as the regular pediatrician had gone into the Army, and this, I figured, was all to the good. A new broom sweeps clean.

When we went into the office he smiled warmly at Susan and said, in a hearty voice, "Well! And what's your name, young lady?"

"Arabella," said Susan, and walked over to look out the window.

Then, behind Susan's back, the doctor and I went through a little pantomime. He raised his eyebrows questioningly and I shook my head hopelessly. Then he put his finger to his lips and shook his head, signalling me to contain myself.

The doctor advanced toward Susan. "Now, now," he said playfully, "that's make believe, isn't it? What's your real name, really and truly?"

Susan turned from the window. "You mean, cross my heart and hope to die?"

The doctor nodded and beamed, casting me a side glance of ill-concealed triumph.

"I'm Carl Haycox," said Susan, and looked him right in the eye.

A half-hour later we left the office with Susan waving a

cheery good-by. On the elevator she said smugly, "I fooled *him* about who I was, didn't I?"

"Yes, my fine feathered friend," I thought to myself, "you're going to fool yourself right into an institution one of these days." The downward plunge of the elevator was in exact accordance with my mood.

The doctor called back that evening and said her hearing was perfectly normal and, in his opinion, she was just being perverse. He advised letting things ride along and, if she persisted in acting stupid and telling lies, to take her to a psychiatrist. The word "lies," he added charitably, was an ugly word and what he really meant was that she could or would not distinguish truth from fantasy. Then, too, there might be all sorts of things that might account for her behavior. She was afraid of or disliked the teacher, something unpleasant had happened in school, she was jealous of her younger sister, she had an inferiority complex, she was an escapist, or—here he hesitated delicately—there was an unhappy home background. But, taken all in all, he thought she would suddenly snap out of it by herself. Children sometimes got little quirks that ironed themselves out, without rhyme or reason.

So I let things ride along. If Susie had been unhappy I would have hesitated but she really looked forward each night to the next day. And I tried to tell myself that I was glad— *glad* that she was an imaginative child, that it was the dreamers in the world who had invented the telephone, the radio, the airplane. I refused to wonder how she might accomplish anything when perhaps she'd never get past the first grade. *First* grade? Horrors, there was no gilt-edged guarantee that she might not flunk kindergarten!

But just when I'd get my morale built up again, along would come Mrs. Newcomb with more details about Darlene's progress. Darlene had been the monitor to the lavatory for two weeks straight; she was to recite a poem at the next P.T.A. meeting; she invariably had her drawings thumbtacked to the bulletin board. (She, Darlene, had no vicious surrealist in her. *Her* stick people never had arms branching out from the waist, nor an indiscriminate number of fingers on one hand as did my child's. One of Susan's drawings, in particular, was seared forever in my memory: a degenerate work of art depicting an egg-shaped creature with an elaborate purple navel!)

So all right. I'd relinquish that dream about Susan being artistic, but why, oh why, couldn't she at least spout poetry à la Darlene? Why did it have to be nothing but hot ball, as played fast and furiously by the class of '56 over at good old Benjamin Franklin? My corroding envy and humiliation lay like a cold stone in my bosom.

When the Christmas holidays arrived I threw myself into the festivities with a somewhat hysterical abandon. "Eat, drink, and be merry," I thought, "for this may be the last joyous Christmas we'll know." Final report cards and "passing" were, I knew, just around the corner, and how live down the ignominy of having one's child repeat kindergarten? I could see my husband saving face by tendering his resignation quickly before the university board might request it; I could see my friends carefully tiptoeing around the subject. Our world would come to an end, not with a whimper but with a bang.

When the dreaded day arrived I opened Susan's report card. At first the words blurred before me, but finally I made it out. It read, in that same elfin library hand: "Susan has been a different child this past month. She is interested, quick to respond, and doing excellent work. She is now advanced to Unit One."

Unit One! I rolled it over on my tongue, savoring the full glory of it all. My child was *not* a moron. It was like a last-minute pardon from the governor; it was like having the doctor say: "Oops, I made a mistake. You don't have leprosy, just the three day measles." It was a miracle of miracles, in a generation that no longer believed in the miraculous.

With winged feet I rushed to the telephone to call my husband. "Hmmm," said he in his calmest and most professorial tone, "have *you* noticed any difference in her lately?"

"No, no, I haven't," I said reluctantly, the glory beginning to fade somewhat. "But then, I haven't asked her anything lately." I put down the receiver and walked out to the kitchen where Susan was thoughtfully smothering a piece of bread with peanut butter.

"Susan," I said casually, "been doing anything special in school lately?" (I sent up a quivering little prayer—"Not hot ball, dear Lord, not hot ball.")

Susan pressed another piece of bread down on top of the peanut butter like a bricklayer plying his craft. She scooped away the oozed-out peanut butter with her finger and licked it off. "Oh, poems and stuff," said Susan, and then added, in kindly fashion, "want to hear one?"

I could only nod my head, afraid to shatter with any words this cozy little camaraderie 'twixt Mother and Daughter. Standing in front of the refrigerator and brandishing the sandwich in winsome gestures she recited:

> "I always like to think that I
> Am just as sweet as apple pie
> And gentle as a summer breeze
> That blows so softly through the trees.
>
> "And so it makes me very sad
> When someone tells me I've been bad.
> Although there may be some truth in it
> I don't admit it for a minute!"

There was a hushed silence as she finished. All of Darlene's past recitals paled beside the superior rendition of this one; all the rancors of the past melted away in this moment of triumph, this triumph of the Fine Arts over hot ball.

I finally pulled myself together and began to prepare the young scholar's lunch. And as I dreamily stirred the tomato soup, I meditated—with a heart filled with bewildered thanksgiving—on the inscrutable ways of God and little five-year-old children.

The Pigtail Stage

No ONE would ever think of me, the mother of three children, as an adolescent. An adolescent has a certain colt-like charm, a refreshing artlessness, a wide-eyed receptiveness. Just the term *adolescence* conjures up a picture of a tight rosebud just beginning to unfurl. That is not me, definitely. If I ever *was* a rosebud, I unfurled long ago.

But adolescence also has another side to it, not quite so appealing. Awkwardness. Giggles and tears. Teeth braces and red nail polish. A smart-alecky brashness. A sensitive unsureness. Dreams of Glory clashing with the fear of being laughed at.

The girl is growing up and, in the process, she can be very, very difficult to stomach.

This second image of adolescence, bear in mind. It is what I mean when I say that I am an adolescent in the process of growing up in Catholicism.

The odd part of all this sudden awareness is that, up to five years ago, I considered myself a mature and well-versed Catholic! As converts went, I guess I even thought I was quite a gladsome addition to Mother Church. And when certain people said: "You're the intellectual type—yours was an intellectual conversion," I smiled deprecatingly but didn't argue the point at all.

Either I did a beautiful job of covering up my colossal ignorance or else those certain people themselves didn't realize the depth and the richness of the inexhaustible gold mine that *is* the Church. There was the gold mine all the time and there also was I, with my little sieve, just playing around with the gold dust. No nuggets.

Some converts, like Chesterton, enter the Church after years of study, brooding, inward struggling, but I have no such story. *Mine* was a whirlwind courtship. *I* was twenty-one ("But I was one-and-twenty, no use to talk to me") and alone in my searching. I was too old to have a Santa Claus acceptance of Catholic doctrine but too young (and impatient!) to give it a seasoned and profound and judicious weighing. Not for me any tortuous exploration from Aristotle down to Maritain. Not for me the hunched figure of "The Thinker." *I*, with the Baltimore Catechism in hand, took instructions for one whole month (I laugh hollowly) and, at the end of that time, I was ready to be knocked over like a ten pin.

I prefer to think that I didn't rush into it like an idiot. It is much more pleasant to think that I, through no grace of my own or any hard work, was just one of the lucky ones. (Christ walks through the crowd, tapping first one and then another, handing them the gift of faith. I got tapped.)

Well, faith is fine—I heartily approve of it!—but faith without much knowledge has to be 100% fool-proof to weather the storm. I, at twenty-one, had no experienced weather eye. *My* barometer was permanently set for: "Fair and sunny weather. Possible light zephyrs from the Gulf coast."

I accepted, with complete faith, the Church as the true Church. Its historical pedigree left me speechless. Ergo, if I believed it to be true, then all I had to do—in the leisure years before me—was to digest more slowly and carefully all the doctrine I had swallowed in one gulp. It was all going to be *very* simple. True, the priest left me with this parting ominous injunction: "You are obliged to keep learning, and the more you learn the more will be expected of you." I didn't realize it but he was pronouncing a life sentence.

I entered the Church blithely. Surely, surely, I had *most* of it under my hat. Ah, I was like a child splashing around the edge of a pool. I didn't realize that out toward the middle of that pool the water got very, very deep. I didn't know that I'd need water wings (at least!) even to begin to figure out a simple phrase like: "Through Him, and with Him, and in Him." About the only phrase that I could understand was the opener: "I will go in unto the altar of God, unto God, who giveth joy to my youth."

I didn't know that one day I'd go beyond the "I" and "my", trying to understand the Mystical Body: the Christ-in-me, the Christ in my neighborhood grocer, the Christ in some unknown and far-away Bengalese housewife. And I certainly didn't dream that one day that Mystical Body doctrine would leap out of the textbooks and right into my life: that I would belong to a Blessed Martin study group, composed of six white members, and six Negro members. Meeting in each other's homes, studying our religion together, becoming good friends over the years . . . ah, this "doing" proved a far better teacher than any fancy textbook.

Nor did I dream that one day I would be in a discussion group, up to my ears in an undreamed-of-world of Catholic thought—liturgy, scholastic philosophy, ethics, and apologetics. I never dreamed that I, Mrs. Hasley, would be batting out choice little assignments like—well, proving, through reason, the immortality of the soul. (I chew my pencil, I absently twist a lock of hair. My soul, poor thing, what is it, to begin with? Is it my mind, my heart, my personality, or a vague sort of balloon situated somewhere around my appendix?)

Ah, converts, join a study club. There's nothing like it. ("Having a wonderful time. Wish you were here. X marks the spot where we had a picnic today.") It's a fascinating business and I can't help feeling sorry for the convert who stops short. They, the stop-shorters, are like people who eat canned soups . . . year in, year out . . . without realizing that a home-made stew is much more delicious and fortifying. Of course, the can opener is easier.

I am not now speaking of the truly simple souls. I would no more hand that little old lady over there, saying her beads, a copy of the *Summa* than I would hit her over the head with it. No, I envy those souls who barely know the fundamentals but have a faith that never questions, never ponders. Just operates. I even envy a certain pious elderly gentleman I know who, with child-like candor, always drinks his cup of coffee before going to Communion. These are Babes in the Wood, and Christ has always shown a great and somewhat disconcerting partiality for children.

What is, I wonder, the status of the not-so-simple convert who has faith but still ponders and questions and keeps stubbing his toes? Is it his fault that, at the time he embraced Catholicism, he didn't realize all there was to embrace?

Born Catholics seem to love converts, stubbed toes and all. They all but reach out and pat them tenderly. But I have a sneaking suspicion that there are many converts who need, not a pat but a good shove. They have gone tepid. The glow and the drama and the novelty of being a convert wear off as one gradually gets bored with the same limited fare, the same old "canned soup." The early enthusiasm and high generosity evaporate as one learns, first hand, that various virtues . . . that look so splendid on the printed page . . . carry a mighty stiff price tag. (Sometimes, alas, we find a convert who never had the glow and the generosity to begin with. His was a marriage of convenience to the Church, not a love affair. Just the term "embraces Catholicism" implies that love should be there. But I'm not talking about these quislings from the Protestant ranks; I mean the honest convert.)

Before joining, it was permissible—nay, commendable—to ask ruthless questions, but after the official plunge the convert hesitates. He's supposed to be an honest-to-goodness member now, no longer a seeker. A question, a doubt, smacks of sabotage.

My advice (hard-earned) to that convert is: *Still be a seeker.* Don't try uneasily to smother those vague, uncertain doubts but drag them out in the open and flog the daylight into them. Otherwise your faith may peter out like a lamp with a dwindling supply of oil. Give the Church a fair chance to prove its claims. It can not only make good its claims but lead you into green pastures, onto broad highways, and along hidden sideroads of pure delight. Not to mention all the interesting fellow explorers you'll meet along the way. (P. S. There is no secret fraternity handclasp involved but neither is there any difficulty in spotting, twenty paces off, a fellow explorer.)

Do I sound, by now, as if I were Moses himself, stone tablets in hand? Oh, there are lots of things that I'm still gnawing away on: free will; the suffering of children; the difficulty of "abandonment" to a Divine Providence that often resembles a crazy quilt design; why "good" Catholics aren't more Christ-like. These are problems to make anyone pause but, look, I was stopped cold on one of the easiest things in Catholicism. The saints.

I took great pains not to investigate them because I was afraid to overstrain my credulity. I was satisfied with the sketchy tidbits I had picked up to let well enough alone. St. Francis loved birds, St. Patrick *didn't* love snakes, St. Thérèse was partial to deluges of American Beauty roses, Blessed Martin was fond of field mice, St. Teresa sailed through the air, the Curé d'Ars lived on stale potatoes, St. Catherine of Sienna bossed the Popes around, St. Anthony ran the Lost and Found Department. Well . . . !

With a blithe sweep of the hand, I relegated the whole batch of them to the parochial classroom: Superman stuff for the eighth graders. But, hold on tight! That sweep of the hand also included the Queen of Saints. I graciously accepted all the doctrine pertaining to Mary (let her have her Immaculate Conception, her Assumption) but I remained coolly aloof in the best Protestant fashion. No devotion. I gazed in bafflement at those who "fled to Mary."

Who said I had to pray to Mary if I didn't want to? Mary, for me, was buried fathoms deep beneath a cloying sentimentality. Mary was an extraneous devotion, suitable mainly for the month of May. I could take her or leave her, December *or* May.

I left her. But one day I found her. One fine day I mentioned this blind spot—oh, so casually—to a priest that I greatly admired. I rather expected him, I guess, to tear the Roman collar off with one strangled gesture, roll up his sleeves, and pitch in. Instead he (wise as a serpent, gentle as a dove) merely said, cozily: "*I* couldn't get along without Mary."

Period. End of apologetics. So instead of him rolling up *his* sleeves, I rolled up *mine*. I found what I needed in a slim little book called *The Reed of God* by Caryll Houselander. It was written, she said, for those to whom Mary is merely "the madonna of the Christmas card, immobile, seated forever in the immaculately clean stable of golden straw and shining snow." For me, Mary—on the Christmas card—came to life.

It is lucky for me that Our Lady doesn't hold grudges. I don't understand how these things operate, but it did seem that, from the moment I apologized to Mary, there began a vast unrolling.

The saints stepped out of the pages of Henri Ghéon's hagiographies, smiled, and said: "Surprise! We're more than a musty relic, a tinted statue, a holy card book mark. We're *real*."

And then I heard someone refer to St. Francis de Sales as the patron of Catholic writers. (I was a Catholic and I was a so-called writer but the two didn't hitch very well.) I figured a little apple-polishing wouldn't come in amiss and so I read his *Introduction to the Devout Life*. Lord love us, St. Francis seemed to have big ideas for me *and* the butcher *and* the baker *and* the candlestick maker. You didn't need a Roman collar or a black veil; your uniform could be either overalls or an apron or a Sloppy Joe sweater. And I began feebly to grasp that a devout life meant more than just slinging your envelope regularly into the collection basket. More than just signing the Legion of Decency pledge. More than attending Sanctuary Society bridge parties and lugging home innumerable door prizes.

More books followed; books with titles that once scared me off. But this is not intended as a plug for Better Books Week. It is true that you won't get far by sticking to the Elsie Dinsmore type of religious best seller, or just riding along on book *reviews*, but that's not my point. All I'm saying is that here was a case of seeking and finding. Generally this refers to the more lofty plane of praying, but perfect prayer, higher contemplation, are way beyond me. (Adolescents have a hard time sitting still and listening; they wiggle and squirm around.)

For some of us, the way must be through reading. How desire what you know nothing about? How meditate if the cupboard is bare? How apply Catholic principles to current problems when you don't understand even the *terminology* of either?

As a convert once wrote me: "I feel as if I had taken out naturalization papers in a strange country. I don't even know how to speak the language."

Christ understands all languages but he doesn't answer questions out loud. (Which is not to say that he doesn't answer.) Perhaps he's standing close by when your hand reaches out for that rental book. What will it be? At the impartial rate of 3¢ a day, you can choose either *Forever Amber* or *The Power and the Glory*. You can pluck either a weed or a flower.

Maybe this is where Christ steps in. Maybe he's whispering: "Go on, take that one, it's good. It'll clear up those loose ends for you. What difference if someone on the bus notices the title and smiles at you? You'll have the last smile. And then that book up on the top shelf (yes, that plain one, with no blurb jacket) would jar you loose from your lukewarm mediocrity. Don't you think you could use that, my friend?"

Of course I'm just imagining Christ in a book shop. I wouldn't really know how it works. I'm just an adolescent. But this adolescence is an awkward stage, and the sooner I can pin up my pigtails and stay up late with the grownups, the better I'll like it.

The First Year

W HEN Susan entered the first grade over at Holy Cross School, I was somewhat apprehensive. Susan is a child one can well be apprehensive about under even favorable circumstances, and here we were starting off with one strike against us already. We were registering one month in arrears of the other young scholars.

The other young scholars would already have mastered the basic principles of classroom etiquette, and I didn't know whether the nun would patiently tutor Susan on the side or let her catch on as catch can. If it were going to be on the catch system, I could already visualize Susan bumbling about uncertainly, if not actually committing minor atrocities, within the portals of Holy Cross.

As a convert mother, I knew as little about parochial schools and nuns as did Susan, and I therefore wasn't qualified to send her off with any sage little Mother-Daughter pep talk. I was reasonably sure that one said "Yes, Sister," instead of "Yeah, Ma'm" but, aside from that, I had little to offer. I could but pay the tuition, send her off with clean ears and a fresh hanky, and send up a prayer that her baptismal innocence would serve her well.

I, myself, at home base, caught on quite rapidly. Tuesday you sent savings stamp money, Friday you sent recess milk money, and in between times you sent pennies for the children's "Mile of Pennies" for the new convent. When it rained it meant solid session, with Susan bouncing back home at one o'clock: mine, all mine, for the rest of the day.

I secretly suspected the nuns of slipping a petition for rain into their morning prayers, and so I, although greatly out-numbered, started slipping a counter order into mine. You have simply no idea how the fervor of my prayer life im-proved, especially during the tricky month of April.

But I *couldn't* cope with the saints and their feast days. Every other week, or so it seemed, good old Holy Cross would spring a holiday on me. Some of these I located, and con-firmed, on the Eucharistic calendar; the others were appar-ently dedicated to obscure, jolly, holiday-loving saints, un-known to the mere layman. I finally decided I might just as well throw my pretty calendar away and abandon myself, willy-nilly, to whatever the fates might send. After that, life was much simpler, if no more serene.

And as for Susan. Well, her orientation proved—shall we say?—interesting. At first she was very non-commital about her academic life, and all my forebodings began to gather into a dark ominous cloud. I wasn't forgetting, for one little minute, her lurid kindergarten career at Benjamin Franklin. Was it possible that Catholics, too, went in for hot ball? One day I summoned the courage to pin her down. "Susan," said I, firmly, "what are you studying in school?"

Her answer was to the point and carried tones of infinite disdain. "Oh, just *God*," she said. I was given clearly to under-stand that she entertained only a vast weariness for first grade metaphysics.

But gradually "just *God*" began to carry with it a great fascination. She would burst into the house with, "Mama! Do you have a mortimal sin?" Or, "Mama! I can talk Latin just like the priest!" The first question was well within the realm of probability, but this latter statement I questioned. When pressed for more details about her linguistic prowess, it ap-peared that she was learning "Do-re-mi-fa-so-la-te-do" in sing-ing class. *Te Deum* . . . do-re-mi . . . what were the odds? This do-re-mi, however, had limited vocal possibilities, but not so the other songs. She got up in the morning singing, tonelessly, " 'Tis the month of our muth-er-er" and went to bed still chanting.

She also developed a sudden and unaccountable interest in

our financial status. For awhile she kept saying, "Mama, are we rich or poor?" and I kept saying, "We're medium." This didn't seem to satisfy and finally she said, with a small note of desperation, "Well, then, which would you *rather* be . . . rich or poor?" When I said "Rich," with no visible hesitation, Susan shook her head reprovingly. "God loves poor people best," she said gravely. Only by a detailed account of all the charitable works I would sponsor, *if* rich, did I raise myself in Susan's estimation.

At Christmas time her piety had reached such an exalted pitch that when I took her down to see Santa Claus, temporarily holding forth in Robertson's department store, she requested a crucifix. There was a little silence and then Santa —with a rather helpless wave of his hand toward the other toys—said, "That's fine, my girl, but nothing else?"

"Anything else you like," said Susan graciously, and with admirable detachment, "but first of all a crucifix. It's gotta be big and it's gotta be blessed."

At which point Santa hastily shoved her off his lap and grabbed up a more normal and reasonable child: a bright little lad who demanded only a Diesel engine, a race horse, and a Daisy rifle.

Next, I encountered the formidable problem of Sister Says.

"Sister says," announced my daughter, "that if you put up a picture of the Sacred Heart in the living room, nothing bad can ever happen to our family. The house won't burn, lightning won't hit us, and none of us will ever get sick."

With Susan pulling down an E (excellent) in first grade Christian Doctrine, I hesitated to tangle with her but, surely, the Sacred Heart carried no such gilt-edged guarantee? It was better by far than anything the Metropolitan Life Insurance Company put out, but I had a hunch that what Sister says gets a good deal of juvenile kicking around.

Next I noticed that Susan's appetite seemed to be falling off. I inquired the reason for this bird-like approach to her victuals.

"Sister says," began Susan patiently, "that I'm to be Jack-in-the-Box in our next play. Sister says she wants me to stay little enough to get in the box. Sister says for me not to dare *grow*."

Well, this battle between Sisters Says and Mother Says (with mother definitely the underdog) sometimes waxed fierce, but there was no denying that the nuns were doing a wonderful job in instilling the faith that moves mountains. There was also, I might add, nothing picayunish in my child's response.

Came the day when Susan, filled with compassion for the Suffering Souls in Purgatory, wanted to fill out a list of our relatives (dead) to drop in the All Souls' box. So, dutifully, I supplied her with a working list: Uncle Albert, Aunt Hattie, Cousin Timothy . . . oh, there were plenty of souls in the family that could use a little heave-ho. But what actually appeared on Susan's list? A grand roll call: St. Thomas Aquinas, the Little Flower, St. Anthony, and St. Francis. Susan had decided to let our parish priest pray for some really worthwhile characters. Pooh to *our* relatives. Let *them* languish.

Interested only in the welfare of the saints, Susan also let *me* languish. On one happy occasion, however, I *did* merit a prayer. One night, saying her prayers, she suddenly lifted her head and said casually, "Could *you* use a Hail Mary for anything?" Indeed I could, thanks, and Susan delivered the goods. Then the head lifted again, speculatively: "Mama! What're you going to use that Hail Mary for?" (Money in the bank; mine—all mine—to spend; but the depositor wants to know *how*.)

Next we went through the holy card stage, and I say "we" because I was the one who was always fishing them out between the davenport pillows or out of the cold air registers. But it was, on the whole, as serious a project as any philatelist's, and Susan and her friends would gather in her bedroom and pore gloatingly over their respective collections. For staying after school and cleaning the blackboards and pounding the chalk out of the erasers, they gained two holy cards apiece. A good deal of bargaining and swapping took place among these young janitors, and a rigid system of evaluation was soon established. All cards with the baby Jesus on were of the highest premium, the Blessed Mother ran a close second, while a mere St. Lucy came dirt cheap.

But gradually the baby Jesus began to lose ground . . . now the Blessed Mother was coming into her own. I didn't realize to just what an extent until the day when Susan and I went downtown shopping for a birthday present. Ethel Schmitt, the little Lutheran girl down the street, was having a birthday party, and it was all settled that we were going to buy her a copy of *Bambi.* But in the book shop Susan, fingering over some books, suddenly gave a piercing shriek. "Oh, buy this," she cried, "It's Blessed Mother!" Indeed it was Blessed Mother—a devotional book on Our Lady of the Snows —but I didn't feel it was quite, *quite* the thing for our little Lutheran friend.

"No. *Bambi,*" said I.

"No. Blessed Mother!" wailed Susan, and I had to drag her out of the shop feeling like a first class heathen. (We finally bought Ethel some carnation bubble bath crystals. 'Twas ever thus . . . the eternal compromise between high principles and the flesh.)

But please understand that I was gratified, on the whole, with Susan's spiritual ardor and high principles, for only at times did it become slightly stifling. And I was proud beyond measure when she brought home from school, near the end of the term, a heart-warming note from Sister Angela. It read, in Sister Angela's neat, flowing script, "Susan has been selected to carry the Blessed Mother's crown of flowers in the May Procession next Friday. I would like her to wear black patent slippers and a blue organdy dress. You can make her a simple little wreath of flowers from your garden."

Well, this was May, 1944, and there happened to be a little world war going on. I gave the note a little shake to see if possibly—just possibly—Sister had enclosed a shoe coupon. Nothing fluttered to the floor, of course, but—even if it had —had Sister tried lately to locate any patent leather? And did Sister know that blue organdy had apparently expired with the first lend-lease agreement? And as for my "garden" that Sister so blandly referred to! There had been heavy rains all week (despite my prayers) and my "garden" consisted of mud-splashed lilies-of-the-valley and some brownish, water-logged snowballs along the east side of the garage. They would, I knew, look utterly charming in a wet and muddy wreath, made by loving hands at home.

I was about to give up before I'd even started on this treasure hunt, and then I reconsidered. This was Sister Angela speaking, and she was not one to be thwarted by shoe coupons, lend lease, or a heavy rain. Very distinctly I recalled the saga of Sister Angela and the Rat.

I had gone over to Holy Cross one afternoon around four-thirty to see her about the forthcoming Christmas play. (I *had* been feeding Susan but was she still small enough to be Jack-in-the-Box?) When I turned the corner of the corridor, leading to the first grade room, I immediately sensed that all was not well. There was an undefinable air of suspense, an unnatural calm. Several nuns stood huddled dolefully around the chapel door, one fingering her rosary.

I stopped and said (quietly, just in case there *was* a wake going on): "Is Sister Angela around?"

"Sister Angela," said one of them, in the barest whisper, "is killing a rat." Just then there came some heavy thud-thuds from the first grade room. The sister winced. "With a broom," she added.

I hate rats. They are big sleek furry beasts with little red eyes and long pointed fangs, and I have heard tell they'll stand up on their hind legs and fight back to the bitter end. But I went slowly down the hall, as if drawn by an evil magnet.

I peered cautiously into the room and, sure enough, there was Sister Angela, broom in hand. But was this the little Sister Angela I saw in Church every Sunday, her black veil pulled modestly forward, her gentle face lowered over her big black beads? *This* Sister Angela had her sleeves and her heavy, voluminous skirts pinned up at strategic points, and she was scowling fiercely.

I politely inquired about the rat. Was the killing a *fait accompli?*

"It's disappeared into thin air," she said crossly. "It must be the devil himself. All the sisters ran away . . . *you* stand guard at the door while I poke around."

I stood guard at the door (after all, what had my Confirmation meant if not to be a Little Soldier?) but poised, as it were, for a quick sprint if necessary. But the rat, or Beelzebub, had sprinted first and was probably even now leering at us from some secret foxhole. Sister carefully and fearlessly covered the entire room, thrashing around in cupboards and wastebaskets, and then gave up. Muttering beneath her breath that it must, indeed, be Beelzebub himself, she started to unpin her skirts.

Suddenly she clutched her hip with a strangled little scream. "He's here! He's here! I've got him!" she called, and there was only a trumpeting triumph in her voice. No fear. Poor Beelzebub had ill-advisedly leaped into her skirts for refuge and nestled cosily on her hip, little realizing he was no match for a Child of Light. A Child of Light who, with her dainty hands, choked the creature.

That was Sister Angela. Small wonder that I felt an honest and genuine awe merely gazing at her signature on the note. With Sister Angela in charge, neither I nor Beelzebub had a chance.

On the day of the May Procession Susan wore black patent slippers (borrowed), a blue organdy dress (borrowed), and a dainty wreath of flowers (75¢) from the local florist.

It was my first May Procession, and it was lovely. (The nuns and I, in unison at last, had prayed for sunny weather and received same.) I even enjoyed " 'Tis the month of our muther-er" as the children walked down the aisle singing it. Somehow, it sounded different from the home version that I had been hearing all year. And Susan—forgive me!—looked completely out of this world as she walked slowly along, bearing the crown. It rested on a blue satin pillow with ribbon streamers leading from each corner. It was a charming bit of pageantry *but* at the end of each streamer was one of Susan's attendants who might, with the slightest jerk or sneeze, knock the crown from the pillow.

I strained my neck in torture as they made their perilous way to the side altar; mine was the agony of the helpless on-looker, in the face of impending doom. But she made it. (And afterwards, when I confided my mental strain to Sister Angela, she gave me a little "O-you-of-little-faith" smile. "Ah," said she, "I had it anchored with four safety pins." So my child had come in on a pin and a prayer. . . .)

At the tiny crowded side altar, Susan knelt with the pillow while Father Mahoney, practically on top of her, blessed it with several vigorous jerks of the holy water sprinkler. Susan, gazing upward, looked like a Michelangelo cherub.

That night, when it was all over, I said to her fondly, "And what were you thinking of, dear, while you were kneeling before Father Mahoney?" (What were you thinking of, my little one . . . seraphim caroling 'round the Eternal Throne?)

"I was afraid he was going to conk me one with that sprinkler," said the little Michelangelo cherub.

Confession and Me

For years I approached confession as blithely as if I were sauntering out to pluck field daisies. As far as I could see, it was one of the easiest things on the Catholic calendar; it was even, for a convert, somewhat disappointing in its simplicity. No hair-shirts, no ashes, no nothing. You just marched in, got it off your chest, and marched out. Simple.

When I read stories about uneasy souls suffering from something called "scruples," I was fascinated. There was, for example, the elderly Miss Tessie in *Pride's Way* who devoted all Saturday afternoon to getting shriven. No sooner would our Miss Tessie emerge from the confessional than a new scarlet sin, a new knife-like doubt, would assail her. Back to the end of the line she would trot, girding herself for a repeat performance: "Bless me, Father, for I have sinned. I made my last confession five minutes ago. . . ."

This was fiction, of course, and good for a laugh, but soon real cases reached my ears. There were Catholics, it seemed, whose insides curled up because of the have-I-broken-my-fast phobia: inadvertently swallowing a gnat (not gluttony!), chewing a fingernail, using Vick's nosedrops, munching a toothpick, having a snowflake melt on one's lip. Not to mention the elusive drop of water (did it or did it not slide down the gullet?) from one's toothbrush.

All my calloused mirth at the expense of these harassed souls was before I, in person, came down with an elegant case of scruples. I found out for myself that it was worse, far worse, than the time I had flu and yellow jaundice, combined, back in 1927. Yet this time no one put me to bed, no one stroked my hot, moist brow, no one said I would ultimately recover. They left me to die like a dog.

So, little Miss Fix-It here started doctoring herself by lugging home big books from the library. The most comforting diagnosis I could wring from the spiritual doctors was that scruples were a "mental aberration." This was just ducky. Was I supposed to order the patrol wagon to back up to the front door? In preference, I decided to lug home MORE books. It was unthinkable that I, a literate and reasonably intelligent citizen (albeit temporarily aberrated), couldn't cure myself. Goodness knows there were enough methods at hand.

The favorite seemed to be the Bully Method: "Come, come, my good woman, relax." Next in line was the vague Pious Method: "Say your Rosary and all will be serene." Next, the Whistling-Past-the-Cemetery Method: "Do you honestly feel your sins would hurl you into *Hell*?" (This is intended to bring forth a hearty and merry laugh of denial. For the scrupulous, it merely raises a very neat point.) Worst of all was the Involved Method: "Did the higher part of the soul sufficiently resist the lower part?" (I'd always stupidly thought that a feature of the soul was its oneness. Now, suddenly, I had a soul that was dividing on me like an amoeba.)

I also resented having tricks played on me. I vividly remember one magazine article on scruples with the last sentence, in big bold type, warning me: "DO NOT REREAD THIS. If you cannot resist, you have a pernicious case." (I read it three times, just to get even.)

The case histories in the books left me cold with indignation. *I* wasn't Miss X who worried as to whether the "purple thing around the priest's neck was hanging straight, thus insuring the validity of the absolution." *I* had honest-to-goodness problems. Was *I* hanging straight?

Let me say right here that you don't have to hack your grandmother to pieces with a buzz-saw in order to develop an inflamed conscience. (So don't bother looking up my police record. Very dull: two tickets for overparking.) Scruples, I have gleaned along the way, can arise from purely physical reasons: nerves, insomnia, an infected tooth, adolescence, menopause, overwork. They can arise from spiritual indigestion: reading the wrong books, trying to become a Little Flower overnight. They can arise from a sudden and rude awakening to sins of omission. And whereas to review old sins in the light of new values is not exactly a sedative, the *quickest* way to a padded cell is to doubt your present good intentions.

My first symptoms appeared when my confessor kept saying, "Now is everything perfectly clear?" and I kept coming back, like Little Sir Echo, with "Perfectly clear, Father, *but*" . . .

After the "But" stage, you sink rapidly.

Next I went blind in one eye and couldn't see out of the other. I couldn't tell a mortal from a venial sin even with a microscope. Yet, St. Francis de Sales had said that a mortal sin was as easy to spy as a scorpion crawling across the floor. I was also told to wait for "a bell to ring"; to have the mathematical assurance of "2 plus 2 equals 4." So I looked for scorpions, listened for bells, and went in for first grade arithmetic. But since I operated on the iron-clad principle of "Never give a sucker an even break," it didn't turn out so good.

It reached the point where, obviously, the only sensible confessional procedure was to point out my virtues, not my vices. This would make for brevity if nothing else. The only flaw was that it didn't coincide with the Council of Trent's conception of confession.

My scruples reached the swollen, high-water mark one night in a hospital, the night before a major operation. Putting no stock in the axiom that only the good die young, I knew —absolutely *knew*—that the bells would soon be tolling. I also absolutely knew I wasn't ready. True, I had been to confession only three days before but—glory, seventy-two hours to account for! To play safe, I had previously made the hospital chaplain promise to be on deck for a final, thorough, and last minute absolution. (I was secretly provoked that I couldn't also receive Extreme Unction. If you've got a bad case of pneumonia, okay, but if you're climbing into the electric chair, no. No apparent danger of death, see?)

At 7 p.m. I pushed the buzzer, demanded the priest (he was fifteen minutes late), and was casually informed he was "out." At 8 p.m. the priest still hadn't shown up but the nurse *had*—with a sleeping pill. I swallowed the pill and then settled down, grimly, to fight off its effect. At 9:30 p.m.— still no priest. Help! Murder! Who was I to come through with perfect contrition, for only the saints—said the books!—could achieve same. At 10:30 p.m. all faith, hope, and charity departed. The corridors were dark; everyone else was sound asleep, including—no doubt—that Judas of a priest.

All that was left was to throw myself on the mercy of Christ, but here was the catch. Christ was no longer Christ. To my panicky mind, he was Boris Karloff in *The Monster Strikes Back.*

At 11 p.m. the priest poked his head around the door. Did I greet him with open arms, strewn palms, loud alleluias? I sat up in bed, burst into tears, pointed my finger at him, and bellowed, "Traitor!" Now that absolution was in sight I could afford first to tell him what I thought of him. I then issued careful orders.

"Look," said I between clenched teeth, "if I say a sin is mortal, it *is* mortal. Do not argue. Do not talk me out of it. Do not even comment. Just absolve."

"All right," said the traitor meekly. (In dealing with danger, Mother Church does not demand heroism beyond the call of duty.)

The minute the dove of peace descended, I was a new and radiant person. I lit a cigarette and we chatted—leisurely, happily—for another good hour. What was a touch of mental aberration betwixt friends? He pointed out that conditional absolution can be given even after apparent death. What had been my hurry? Besides, I had asked for a *last minute* absolution, hadn't I?

I survived. The scruples also survived. Didn't I know, by now, just how ridiculous I was acting? Certainly. Even the

insane have their lucid moments and know they're *not*
Napoleon.

With my next relapse, I confided my woes to my best
friend for—said the books!—"trouble shared is trouble
halved." My friend almost collapsed from mirth. "Oh," she
gasped, wiping her eyes, "I'm sorry. It's just the way you *tell*
it. With your sense of humor you couldn't possibly—ha! ha!
—be serious about this."

But I was—ha! ha!—serious. I resolved, then and there, that
if I recovered I would shout out the remedy from the house-
tops. I would become a one-man testimonial bureau.

There is, barring a Lourdes miracle, only one solution for
scruples: cold facts, warmly presented. My heart bleeds for
people who need—not the patrol wagon, not a pat on the
back, not a kick in the pants—but *specific* answers. Poor
souls, they don't even know how to phrase questions.

Thus it is that I nominate for canonization one Reverend
Alfred Wilson, C.P., for his highly entertaining, highly illumi-
nating book called *Pardon and Peace*. *That's* the medicine.
Let the rest of the world have its old penicillin.

Father Wilson lets down his hair with abandon, discusses
both sides of the confessional, and leaves not a stone unturned.
He even tells you where to park your umbrella. Understand,
the saints had the right idea—be God-centered, not self-cen-
tered—but they didn't handle the umbrellas. This British
priest has taken the confessional, turned it inside out and upside down, and shaken it *good*. Out tumble the lax, the tender,
the scrupulous, the calloused, and the "What's it all about,
anyway?" penitents. For all, he rolls away the clouds and
makes spring come busting out all over.

The first sign of spring, for me, was: "No one is obliged
to put himself to serious inconvenience when he goes to confession." (*Inconvenience!* I love the quaint understatements of
some of these theologians. The box, for me, was merely like
stepping into a cement mixer.)

Why *wouldn't* it be like a cement mixer if you felt that
every single word dropping from your palsied lips had to be
painstakingly accurate? According to my logic, everything was

up to *me* (leave nothing to the mercy of God or the brightness of the priest—too risky) and I began on Wednesday to prepare my essay for Saturday.

And beautiful essays they were, too. It was a shame that the priest never had the pleasure of actually hearing one of them. What *he* heard, when the slide went up, was a halting, gasping, sweating, thrashing recitation that bore no resemblance to the original polished manuscript. Even a Curé d'Ars would have been hard pressed to figure out, from the noises, whether I was fish, fowl, or mineral. (Advice: when you reach the gasping fish stage the only way to get off the hook is to be excused from integral confession. Just say, "I am unable to judge the gravity of my sins" and swim away into less troubled waters.)

I'm afraid confession, for me, will never be the good old "plucking daisies" session it was originally, but I'll tell you this much. Even though I do not yet measure up to the ideal penitent ("Be blunt, be brief, be gone"), I can now get through confession without the priest or myself collapsing from the strain.

Pardon and Peace has actually left me so little to worry about that I hardly know what to do with my spare time. I don't *even* have to worry about any possible future trip to Indonesia. When one is traveling abroad, and not able to speak the language, absolution may be received by confession and displaying sorrow by "signs or gestures." Isn't that wonderful?

I also found out something else: I am of some use in the world. Penitents like me are "the direct answer to the priest's prayer: 'Jesus, send me here my Purgatory!'"

Grandma Called It Sloth

Oꜰ ᴀʟʟ the capital sins, I think sloth is the most appealing. I even like the sound of the word itself. Our modern "Get a wiggle on, you big lug," can't compare with the withering elegance of Grandma's "Fie! What sloth, what sloth!"

Sloth is such a cunning little word that I really mourn its passing. The only time I ever run across it is either in a catechism or in an encyclopedia and, needless to say, the encounter is not frequent. The catechism, unfortunately, isn't illustrated (no Man the Sluggard) but the encyclopedia offers one a picture of the Three-Toed Sloth: a charming inert creature, hanging upside down by his toe-nails from the bough of a tree. And that's *all* he does. Just hangs. He has (to continue the zoological lore) coarse long hair in gray or greenish-brown tones, almost indistinguishable from the foliage. He also looks, I might add, absolutely content with his lot and not at all concerned about any catechism.

Perhaps the reason I feel so sympathetic toward this Three-Toed Sloth is that both of us would have driven Grandma crazy. While it is true that I do not hang by my toe-nails from the chandelier, I do—by Grandma's standards—wallow in sloth every morning. Every morning I bring the coffee pot into the living room and settle down in an easy chair to drink coffee and read. It's deplorable. The dishes wait, the beds wait, and—by the time I arise to tackle my chores—the neighbors have far outstripped me. *Their* washing is already flapping in the breeze by the time I'm just wending my way to the basement. It's deplorable. But not half so deplorable as my attitude. My slothful attitude is: "So what? The clothes get washed, don't they?"

Sometimes, of course, my late start means that I am doing manual labor in the afternoon. This is very bad. No real lady would consider it for a split second; only poor white trash, I am told, do housework in the afternoon. Once again, my attitude is deplorable. I think: "So what? Just call me Tobacco Road Ellie."

These are surface attitudes. Underneath is the very real conviction: "What difference does it make if my neighbor gets her washing hung out first? Particularly, what difference will it make fifty years from now? But my Catholic reading, that I squeeze into the early morning, *will* make a difference to me fifty years hence."

Very edifying, you may think suspiciously, but why—pray—not face my state of life duties first and *then* read?

Well, it's like this. (1) I'm a sluggard. I *like* to stall. (2) That blessed session after breakfast (the girls off to school, the baby back to bed) is the one time of the day when the house is peaceful. Why be a dope and squander the peace? (3) That blessed session after breakfast is the only time of the day when my mind is fairly bright. The wise man reapeth whilst the sun shineth.

I was delighted, some while back, to find these convictions bolstered and approved in a magazine article. This article claimed (and I'm a pushover for scientific data when they serve my purpose) that your brain functions best between the hours of 8:00 and 10.00 a.m. You're supposed to have an efficiency of 105 degrees, whatever that means, at 8:00 a.m., and this efficiency ebbs throughout the day, hitting a low at 4:00 p.m. (Very convenient. That's just when the afternoon paper arrives and I'm all set for the comics.) Then the author winds up with a non-scientific but rather beautiful flourish: "I learned to skim the cream off the day and use the rest for cheese-making."

There you are. Do you think I'm going to waste *my* precious

105-degree efficiency scrubbing the egg off the breakfast
dishes? No, sir! I'm going to sit down with a book and give it
all I've got. I'm going to turn the full brilliance of those
105 degrees on something worth illuminating.

Well, I'd like to leave you with this heroic picture of me in
mind—out after sanctification, hammer and tongs—but
honesty forbids. I read Catholic reading, not to be noble,
not in lieu of a hairshirt, but simply because I enjoy it. Somehow, I find it quite interesting to read about why I'm here and
where I'm going and how I'm doing along the way. Mystery!
Suspense! Clues! It beats a good detective story all hollow.

It was not always thus. Time was when I wouldn't have
endured Catholic reading either before, with, or after my
morning coffee. Catholic reading was something you did for
fifteen minutes daily (eyes on clock) for a Lenten penance.
The nastier the dosage, "the more good it did you." And,
early in the game, I hit some pretty nasty stuff: not bitter-
nasty but syrupy-nasty.

Shortly after my conversion I read a few Catholic novels
and I began to wonder if I'd joined the right church. These
fictional Catholics, filled to the brim with all the solid virtues, were wondrous dazzling but even more wondrous
puzzling. I began to wonder, as I read about these infallible
creatures, just why the Sacrament of Penance had ever been
instituted. Just to take care of me? It seemed kind but scarcely
logical that I should have a sacrament all to myself. Or perhaps Confession was just a quaint old hangover from the
Middle Ages when Catholics occasionally erred?

All in all, these novels were out of the world. They be-
longed in Hollywood, with Ingrid Bergman and Bing Crosby
all ready to step into the leading roles. I finally decided that,
if I had to read about saints, I'd read about real ones. These,
too, were a disappointment. The hagiographies I hit ran like
this: "Saint So-and-So's heart burned with such a great love
of God that it scorched his shirt." Or, "Anastasius, a Persian
monk, was beheaded for the faith in 628; he is invoked against
headaches."

(The sensitive interpretation, the profound insight, the keen weighing of Catholic values! Poor saints. They had rugged going on earth and—if one could suffer in Heaven—these biographical gems would be a final crucifixion.)

Next I tried some straight spiritual reading, and this was *my* final crucifixion. The author tried hard to make me feel like a worm and succeeded only too well. All I wanted was to crawl down into the nearest cesspool, obviously my natural habitat, and call it quits.

I don't remember how or when the *good* Catholic reading began to creep up on me, but creep it did. It crept up like the tide, covering the barren shore. The tide brought in the Catholic topnotchers: Chesterton, Charles Péguy, Caryll Houselander, Graham Greene, Evelyn Waugh, François Mauriac, Walter Farrell, Gerald Vann, and other sterling souls. *These* authors wrote with integrity: wrote about real people (neither angels or worms) with real problems in a real world. *These* authors were my undoing. They were too blamed absorbing.

So, heed these confessions of a sluggard. Remember, the first downward step is to pick up a good Catholic book. The second horrible step is to forget yourself and read past the allotted fifteen minute stint. The safest and simplest thing is to steer clear of the whole business, or you, too, may fall prey to the insidious delights of sloth.

* * * * *

P. S. I forgot to mention that there is also such a thing as spiritual sloth. I'm sorry. I certainly meant to get around to it but . . . well, that's a sluggard for you.

To Each His Own

I WANTED, terribly, to be an Apostle. My soul was ablaze
to sally forth and sow apostolic seeds along the highway: to
be a fisher of men, a feminine St. Paul understudy. So-o-o,
the local Catholic apostolic committee—sizing up my talents
—gave me a job. They gave me a job stuffing envelopes.

It became my little apostolate to scan the obituary notices
every evening and speed Catholic consolation, via pamphlets,
to all local bereaved families, regardless of creed. It was a
very worthwhile project, they kept telling me, but it carried
with it very little satisfaction. I never knew what happened to
my pamphlets. It was entirely an I-shot-an-arrow-into-the-air-
it-fell-to-earth-I-know-not-where arrangement. Personally, I put
no stock in the biblical admonition not to let your left hand
know what your right hand is up to.

Too, this business of stuffing a pamphlet into an envelope,
writing out "Miss Sadie Hotchkiss," and licking a two cent
stamp was hardly what you would call creative. The only time
it became at all creative was when the apostolic funds sank
low and I had to whittle down my mailing list. Then I had
the sensitive job of deciding just what families were probably
the least cut up over the bereavement. "H-m-m," I would
think, "here's a guy who was ninety-seven and living with his
sister-in-law. Scratch."

All in all, it was quite a deadly little apostolate: a far cry
from my modest desire to be another St. Paul. I continued to
stuff envelopes but I secretly hoped, like an understudy wait-

ing for the prima donna to come down with laryngitis, for my big chance.

Then my call came. I was asked to give a talk before the Sanctuary Society of St. Benedict's Church. I was asked to take the place of a brush salesman (presenting his wares as a money-raising project for the group) who couldn't make it that evening. I pointed out to the apostolic committee that I'd never given a talk in my life and they pointed out that *surely* I could compete with a brush salesman. At the time I accepted I really thought I could.

Feverishly, I rushed into my preparations. Let the dead bury their dead! Here was my chance to hit those highways! Perhaps my talk to the Sanctuary Society would prove a milestone: a revelation of hitherto untapped abilities. What, I asked myself tremulously, did Msgr. Fulton Sheen have that I didn't have? (And Echo answers: "Plenty." You really don't have to finish reading this to find out the answer.)

I was to talk on Catholic reading, a subject dear to my heart. I would tell these people personally what Catholic reading had meant to me: the stimulation, the satisfaction, the downright pleasure. My enthusiasm would, I thought, make up for any technical drawbacks as a speaker. (All I knew about public speakers was that they always plunked a watch down in front of them and then paid no more attention to it. That didn't seem so difficult.)

I was particularly buoyed up by a passage from Walter Farrell's *Companion to the Summa* and I quote: "Let the lecturer mount the platform armed with a lecture that bristles with practical problems and the audience will yawn him down. If, on the contrary, his intellectual wanderings touch on such things as the essence of an angel, the intellect of a man, or the foundations of the universe, his audience will be straining at the leash like a hound eager to be off after the hare. The mind of man must have mystery because the mind of man must have intellectual food."

Today, after speaking to that Sanctuary Society, I am still fond of Rev. Walter Farrell, but I don't know why. If ever I could, with perfect justice, sue a man . . . !

Anyway, the specific title of my talk was to be CATHOLIC BOOKS YOU'LL LIKE: a blithe, presumptuous title if ever. Have you ever tried to tell an assorted group of strangers just what they'll like? Try it sometime, with my blessing. Maybe your audience *will* strain at the leash like a hound eager to be off after the hare. My audience was eager to be *off*, all right, but . . .

Well, Nature tried her best to stop me. Shortly before my debut, I came down with a heavy cold and developed a guttural voice that made Sophie Tucker sound like a lilting soprano. The show must go on, I told myself hoarsely, and I temporarily abandoned the Faith of My Fathers for Christian Science. I *really* didn't have a cold but (like Mrs. Eddy, who was not above going to the dentist with aching teeth that weren't really aching) I ate cough drops by the handful.

I went around the house practicing my talk, learning to time the laughs and, of course, prepared to stop for any spontaneous bursts of unbridled enthusiasm. My uncooperative family didn't take it half so seriously as I, although my husband did try to cheer me up about the size of my audience. "It's better," said he, "having a large audience like this instead of a small group. Then you won't notice individual faces: it'll just be a big blur. Of course," he added thoughtfully, "it may make you sick to your stomach."

My children weren't any more helpful. They seemed to regard me as still their mother, not a public figure, and kept interrupting my monologue with unreasonable demands for jelly sandwiches or for mislaid galoshes. "Hush, child," I would say. "Mother must be an apostle."

On the night of the talk I drove over to St. Benedict's with a temperature of 100.2, little knowing that all I was to leave with them that night was the virus of the common cold. I was scared, plenty scared, but I had the faith that moves mountains. I scorned reading my paper like an amateur; I was just going to talk easily, persuasively, woman to woman. Still, just to play safe, I had memorized my opening line. I wanted a nifty opening line to hang onto, to serve as a spring-board.

There would, I reasoned, be the standard flattering little

introduction. Something like: "Mrs. Hasley has graciously consented to speak to us this evening on Catholic reading, a subject we are all vitally interested in. A convert, I am sure she will bring us real food for thought. A Catholic writer herself, her qualifications are many," etc., etc. What the qualifications could possibly be, I didn't know, but that was the chairlady's problem.

So, after this fanfare, I would rise, smile, and carefully ad lib: "Thank you. A very nice introduction indeed but you forgot one very vital statistic: namely, that this is my very first talk." My smiling poise would, naturally, give the lie to this, but it would establish a very nice feeling of camaraderie.

God's inscrutable ways of instilling humility and of chastising the wayward are many. This is one. To begin with, picture the cold, dank basement of St. Benedict's. Originally designed, I suspect, by a disciple of Salvador Dali, its labyrinthine ways were enough to shatter the nerves even of a hardened speaker. From a corridor I innocently passed through a door and stepped, all unawares, onto a raised platform overlooking the throng below. It was like one of those little balconies that Mussolini, in his heyday, used to bellow from, and you know what happened to *him*. However, with all eyes on me, I stepped onto this diabolical platform and then descended, like Dante into Hell, a long row of steps. Unfortunately, I did not have the good fortune to slip and break a leg.

As I look back on it, there was a certain stark simplicity about my introduction that was admirable but at the time I couldn't see it. That chairlady merely said briskly: "This is Mrs. Hasley" and then sat down, sending my opening line to Glory.

The faces stared up at me: "What! No brush salesman?" Standing there like a lug, I knew myself for the yellow dog of an apostle I was. I wanted nothing so much as to turn tail and scramble up those steps. Stage fright set in like gangrene and I could feel myself turning a pale, lovely green: a charming foil, if nothing else, for my new red hat. Beneath that red hat was a mind gone completely blank. Shaken by that flight of stairs and now bereft of my cute opening line, I was a lost soul hurtling through space.

I must have opened my mouth and said something because I became aware of a croaking voice seemingly coming from behind the basement pipes. This voice was saying things that had sounded very fine in my own living room but now sounded utterly asinine. It was saying things like, "Spiritual reading is *fun!*" (Spinach is delicious, darling. Take just a teeny bite. See, watch Mama. Yummy!) And my words, with every good reason, were bouncing against a stone wall and right back at me.

Have you ever tried to woo a stone wall? Try it sometime, with my blessing. The faces, incidentally, with spectacles on were the most unnerving: two bits of cold glass gleaming inscrutably. I wouldn't know if all audience faces look like big, blank pumpkins, but this I do know: from now on, whenever I go to a lecture, I'm going to sit in the front row and beam, clap my hands, throw confetti, and whistle through my fingers to encourage the speaker. *That's* my future apostolate.

In two minutes flat I knew, with a crystal certainty, that I was never cut out to be a public speaker. Self-knowledge is fine—nay, a first step toward sanctification—but I maintain that there is a time and a place for such searing revelations.

My talents are limited or I would have, at that point, wiggled my ears, broken into a tap dance, or done card tricks to salvage the evening. Perhaps it was not too late to suggest playing bunco? But no. I had been sent forth to sow apostolic seeds and I was going to sow.

Desperately, I began to pitch book titles at them so fast and furiously that Sheed and Ward's fall book list, read backward, would have been as lucid. Father Farrell had said that the mind of man craves mystery and I was giving it to them.

I was so bogged down in mystery that at first I paid no attention to the little noises. With my knees knocking, my pulse pounding, and my ears ringing, why quibble about a little more racket? But, as it grew louder, I finally caught on. From the open kitchen door there now came the heavy and unabashed clunk of crockery and good, strong whiffs of coffee.

I could imagine the head of the Refreshment Committee turning to one of her underlings and saying: "La! Isn't that dame ever going to quit? Bang the coffee pot a little harder, Myrt."

It was too much. I limped to an end and sat down, the one brilliant stroke of the evening. It was so very brilliant that it even brought forth a faint sprinkling of applause. The applause, in turn, unleashed the Kitchen Committee. They rushed out bearing hot coffee, like an emergency First Aid squad, to revive my audience.

Like a hit-run motorist I fled the scene, not waiting to see if my audience revived or not. All I wanted was to make my un-Samaritan getaway before the stupor wore off and mass hysteria set in.

Today, I am once again back in the obituary department. I am once again stuffing envelopes, and it's a wonderful little apostolate: so quiet, so peaceful, so sheltered. So what if I do get tired of licking those two cent stamps? To each his own, to each his own.

I Like Married Life

Consider, please, my current dilemma-of-the-month.

If I refuse to write this request article on married happiness (complete with ready-made title), the editors will think: "Oho! So the Hasley marriage has gone *pfft*, eh?" If, against my finer instincts, I *do* write it, I am asking for my purgatory here on earth at the hands of my friends. I am quite certain that my friends have never before thought of me in the role of Dorothy Dix, and they may not take to the idea with the proper reverence.

Of course, if this article were merely a matter of giving a brief testimonial like a paid soap ad ("For whiter, longer lastin' suds," says Mrs. Hasley, local housewife, "the married life just can't be beat"), it wouldn't be so bad. But no. *I'm* supposed to give the customers the *real* low-down on what I think of my married life.

And who will read it? Egads! My husband, my mother-in-law, my neighbors, my parish priest . . .

Greater folly hath no woman than to lay down her marriage for friend and foe to inspect. Does my husband beat me in his spare moments; fly into a rage over a missing pajama button; leave his soggy towels on the bathroom floor? Do I dash to the breakfast table with my face swimming in cold cream, my hair in pin curls, and wrapped in a frowzy Mother Hubbard? Do we both snarl at each other, while the coffee percolates, as to who gets to use the Plymouth that day? Does he object to my so-called literary career? If not, why not? And how (cluck of the tongue!) can I possibly find time to write and still do justice to my state of life? (P. S. State of life: Notre Dame faculty wife with one husband, three children, an eight-room house, and no scrub lady.) As to romance, am I *really* glad I got married or am I just keeping a stiff upper lip? And, if happy, would I not possibly have been *more* happy with that cute Harold Snodgrass I went steady with during my junior year in college?

Well, all this sort of eyewash might well be grist for the mills of Ilka (*In Bed We Cry*) Chase, but I figured it would be far safer just to play around with a blow torch and a goodly sized keg of nitroglycerine. In fact, the more I thought about it the more I began to question even the validity of the title for this proposed eulogy.

"And who said I liked married life, pray?" I asked coldly. Naturally, since the editor wasn't within slugging distance, I took it out on my husband. "Marriage is a sacrament, sure, but so are Penance and Extreme Unction. Does that mean you're supposed to *enjoy* them? Marriage, in real life, is a necessary evil . . . to protect one's young, to stabilize society, to lessen concupiscence . . . and let's say no more about it."

I'd had a rough day. My dress that the baby had spilled Cocomalt on had come back from the cleaners with the Cocomalt undisturbed. The water softener had gone on the blink just as I'd started to shampoo my hair. The butcher had sent me a pot roast with a price on its head that would have paid for a new davenport. Several of my best blouses that I had thoughtfully sprinkled and then forgotten to iron were now covered with a light green algae. My husband had gone off that morning on the bus, graciously leaving the car for me to use but absent-mindedly taking the car keys along with him. Danny had hit the new little neighbor boy over the head with his shovel, and the new little neighbor boy's mother had made it very clear to me that the only reason she was staying in such a neighborhood, with its Dead End kids, was because of the housing shortage.

Boiled down, it was one of those days that Father Dowling had warned us about at the Cana Conference—one of those days when the little woman is certain she missed her calling to be a nun, when convent walls look mighty inviting.

"How do I know if marriage is my forte?" I continued, piling it on thick, not letting go, contrary to all Cana Conference rules and regulations. "I mean, I never got a chance to try being a cloistered Carmelite or a grand opera singer or a Powers Girl model or a Pulitzer Prize winner." (Even as I talked, the grass on the other side of the fence kept getting greener and greener.) "Maybe I *would* be better adjusted living alone in a penthouse overlooking the Hudson, with nothing to come between me and my typewriter. Besides, Aunt Gertrude thinks I've got loads of talent. Maybe I could have written the great American novel by now. Who knows?"

"Who knows?" echoed my husband wistfully. Understand, he wasn't feeling wistful about that unwritten novel. No, that was all to the good. It was just that, his soul being a calm and contemplative one by nature, the quiet penthouse idea seemed to have snagged his fancy—not for me but for himself. Anyone with three children who act as if pure jungle blood flowed in their veins will know what I mean.

Unfortunately, we were discussing all this during what Mr. Longfellow so charmingly called "The Children's Hour"— that delightful lull in the day, betwixt the dusk and the daylight, when grave Alice and laughing Allegra and Edith with the golden hair all nestled around Mr. Longfellow's knee and prettily begged for stories. Mrs. Longfellow, I presume, had served supper at four o'clock (or else Alice and Allegra and Edith would have been yapping for food, not stories) and was now washing the dishes.

Be that as it may, all I can say is that the children's hour at our house would have made Mr. Longfellow's beard curl. I had just captured and led Janet to the piano, and so we were having a petulant and furious version of "Down in the Valley." Danny was dumping over the dining room chairs to form a train. Susan, like a tobacco auctioneer, was loudly reciting her catechism: "Are the three Divine Persons really distinct from one another? Yes, the three Divine Persons are really distinct from one another. Are the three Divine Persons perfectly equal to one another? Yes, the three Divine Persons are perfectly equal to one another. Are the three . . ."

Over the din, I shouted to my husband: "Can you give me any hints as to what I might write? Can you think of anything, offhand, in favor of all *this*?" To me, at that moment, it was a mystery that ranked right in there with cosmic rays and Russia's foreign policy.

"No," my husband shouted back, "but if *you* can think of any good answers, I'm willing to correct your spelling and punctuation. And now let's eat; I'm starving. I hope that's not a pot roast I smell, because that's what I had this noon at the cafeteria."

So I got up and went out to the kitchen to poke the pot roast. My alleged helpmate was no more help with menus than he was with my literary career. Obviously, I had but one alternative left: hie myself down to the library and see what the theologians thought was nice about marriage. *They* weren't as close to the subject as I; *they* could well afford a fine detachment. Also, if I could only find my old notes from the Cana Conference (let's see, would they be in the buffet drawer or under the desk blotter or still in my pocketbook?), I might swipe some of Father Dowling's material.

Yep, that conference had really been packed with matrimonial ammunition but, alack, a whole year had since intervened. Personally, I could use a conference just about every other weekend. Maybe other people don't need to be jacked up as often as I but . . . ah, well, we can't all be Strong Characters, can we? The wheat and the tares shall grow side by side until Judgment Day, says Holy Writ.

Actually, after my Cana Conference, I want you to know that this tare was a new woman for almost two weeks before she went back to normal. And during this subnormal period, I *even* wrote a love letter to my spouse, as per Father Dowling's instructions. This letter—saying all the unsaid words of appreciation that, somehow, pile up unsaid over the years —was to be tucked under his cup of coffee or stuck in his hatband. I chose the hatband. As to the letter itself . . . well, if I do say so, it was quite a beautiful contribution to the world of Arts and Letters. I had not only cited his many manly and Rock-of-Gibraltar qualities but I had gone the whole hog. I had forgiven him the Unforgivable Sin.

The Unforgivable Sin, in my books, was the time he brought a strange gentleman home with him without a second's warning. Unfortunately, they caught me—flat-footed—taking a cozy snooze on the davenport, and who (I ask you!) can roll off a davenport and be a suave and scintillating hostess? Especially when your husband identifies the strange gentleman as Bruce Marshall, the novelist, and then wanders casually out to the kitchen for drinks, leaving you to hold the fort. ("Oh, my man, I love him so, he'll never know . . .")

I have since tried to recall anything coherent I may have said to Mr. Marshall, but it's a lost cause. All I remember is saying, suavely, "And do you know Father Gerald Mann in England?" and having my husband call in from the kitchen, "You mean Father *Vann*, dear."

All in all, this was a wound that had not healed easily for, if I'd only had a little warning, I'm *sure* I could have performed more brilliantly. If not along the literary line, I could have at *least* had time to run the vacuum sweeper around.

But all this was water under the bridge. My immediate problem was to collect a lot of edifying material and then, somehow or other, bring it down to the level of 1253 Diamond Avenue. In other words, find a reasonable motive for liking my motley role of scrub lady, wash lady, ironing lady, dietician, cook, nursemaid, police woman, seamstress, impromptu hostess, interior decorator, marketer, plumber . . .

With a loud groan, I appealed once more to the head of the house (and I use the term loosely) for a little assistance. Now that he had devoured most of the pot roast (and wrecked my plans for tomorrow's hash), he might be more amenable.

"Would it be a mortal sin or a venial sin," I inquired, "if I publicly stated that I was crazy about housework?"

"Coming from you," said he, "it would be a statement that would cry aloud to Heaven for vengeance. Anyway, I don't think that was quite what the editor had in mind for you to dwell on. I think he wanted something gay and amusing, something like the married life of William Powell and Myrna Loy in the Thin Man series. Think hard, my darling. What gay and amusing things have happened around here today?"

That last remark, in itself, was enough to make me burst a blood vessel, but his mention of married love in the movies was simply the last straw. Some time ago I had seen "The Bishop's Wife," a flicker calculated to make any normal housewife drool with envy. In this movie, see, lucky Loretta Young has a handsome male angel named Dudley who is always on tap to brighten her days. So she needs someone as a baby sitter? The angel Dudley takes over. So her husband is too busy to take her out to lunch and buy her violets? The angel Dudley takes over. And the beautiful part is that it's strictly on the up and up, for who is going to question the motives of an angel? I, myself, found it a wee bit difficult to think of dark and virile Cary Grant as just pure spirit but, anyway, who couldn't use a couple of Dudleys around the house?

Thoroughly disgruntled with the portion Life had dealt *me*, I decided—as soon as the last child was stowed away—just to go to bed, pull the covers up over my head, and forget the whole trying problem.

After an impassioned plea to St. Jude—who handles Impossible Cases—I finally fell asleep, slipping into a merciful dream world where everything was comparatively simple. In my dream, all I had to do was complete—in twenty-five succinct words—the sentence "I Like Married Life Because," send in a box top of Krispy Kwik-Kooked Krunchies, and win a new Nash.

This was worth fighting for! (Never could win one of the Nashes in the parish raffles, and the Plymouth was falling apart at the seams.) So, working backwards, I cleverly decided to ferret out first what griped me *most* about the daily wear and tear of domestic life and then see what I had left. Way in the lead of gripes were (1) *too much racket* and (2) *lack of solitude*. A runner-up peeve was *picking up after people*.

As I brooded upon these trials, the image of that penthouse overlooking the Hudson came poignantly back to me. Order (not a grand piano misplaced) . . . solitude (ah! the beautiful

meditations I would now be able to cook up) . . . gracious
living (meals sent up on a tray, complete with a yellow tea
rose) . . . and, above all, *quiet!* Oh, there might be the faint
toot of a small tug on the Hudson to pierce the calm of evening, or perhaps the muted call of a nightingale, but I could
put up with this much . . .

It was here that St. Jude, complete with wings, borrowed,
no doubt, took over.

"Who are you trying to fool?" whispered St. Jude. "Why
do you try to cover up the truth with such smart-alecky non-
sense? You know perfectly well you wouldn't be *un*married or
swap your family for anything in the world."

"Of course not," I said indignantly. "Whatever gave you
that . . ."

"Well, then," muttered St. Jude, darkly, "let's have no more
chitter-chatter about penthouses and muted nightingales. And
why do you think the single life automatically means a penthouse? More often, it's a dingy boardinghouse room or a neat,
bleak room at the Y.W.C.A. or an impersonal hotel room.
And let me tell you one more thing . . . I get just as many
desperate appeals from the penthouses as from anywhere else.
Only, they seem to have different complaints. Too *much*
quiet, too *much* solitude, *no* people to pick up after. Is there
no balance on earth? But if people like you would just stop
and think a minute and look around at the next guy . . ."

"Yes, Sir," I said meekly. The possibility of being crossed
off the list of even St. Jude's Impossible Cases was enough to
give me pause. Beside which, I knew I really hadn't been playing fair.

I knew as well as the next housewife that, whereas peace and
quiet were all very fine, peace and quiet could also boomer-
ang into something else. A hellish word. *Loneliness.* It's almost unsporting to bring it up, because, in any discussion of
the married life versus the single life, that is the one word—
the devastating touché—that finishes the bout. It's like saying,
"And did you have a merry Christmas?" to a woman who
spent the day in her hotel room, writing letters and rinsing
out her silk stockings.

Few are the stalwart souls who can buck it alone and like it. Of course, a little loneliness for *everyone* is not only inevitable but good—it throws you back to God—but a loneliness that is empty, not dedicated, a dead end in itself, is perhaps the saddest thing in the world.

With a bouncing and growing family, you don't have a Chinaman's chance to be lonely. You can go crazy from all the hip-hip-hooray, sure, but not from loneliness: not from those "All alone by the telephone" or "I hate to see the evening sun go down" blues. The average mother is generally so tired by five o'clock that she *loves* to see the evening sun go down. Yet there's nothing like being "as a fruitful vine, with thy children as olive plants round about thy table" to dispel any sense of futility or of not being needed or wanted. Also, these olive-plants—since they give a sense of fulfillment—are about the best beauty treatment I know of for a female. What price dishpan hands or a somewhat thickened waistline? Children keep you *young*, a secret that Helena Rubinstein is still hunting around for in her beauty salons.

But let us on to the larger view! Since the most important thing in the world is the salvation of one's soul (and not just getting over the line, either!), let's look at the married life from that angle. To begin with, it's *two* people saving their souls together—not just one—and this, methinks, is a much cozier arrangement. In Christian marriage, with Christ forming a triangle, you get assistance, free (!) spiritual criticism, and the comfort of companionship from one who knows all about you and loves you anyway.

Not—Heaven forbid—that the Nuptial Mass automatically assures one of unsullied bliss here below and eternal bliss upstairs. *Au contraire*, marriage makes one more vulnerable to acute unhappiness (the loss of a child, unfaithfulness of one's spouse) and can also be a keen temptation to sin (birth control, shady business transactions because of economic panic).

Yet, for us ordinary people, marriage is the best *bet* for human happiness and the greatest *natural* means to sanctification. It offers a perfectly marvelous opportunity to die to self. Perhaps no big spectacular cross to lug, but a host of small mortifications that, *surely*, are almost as good as sleeping on a wooden plank, getting up at 2 A. M. for Adoration, or wearing a hair shirt.

And as to the basic virtues! There is nothing like a family to break down one's intellectual pride (discovering you can't even work fourth grade arithmetic any more) or feminine pride (having them tell you that your new dress makes you look heftier) or spiritual pride (suggesting you go out to a movie, that it might improve your foul disposition). And as to selfishness: you learn to share the bathroom, the clothes hangers, the dresser drawers, the telephone, your extra check from Aunt Maude, and eventually (I greatly fear) your silk stockings with your daughters.

But the greatest of virtues, and the most difficult, is to acquire at least a reasonably good imitation of holy patience. Such as getting a child all equipped in snowsuit, mittens, and galoshes and then having him pound on the kitchen door, three minutes later, ready to come indoors again. But my own special crucifixion is to have to put down a good book every two jerks and answer questions, blow up balloons, tie shoe strings, get another cookie, or remove bubble gum from someone's hair. And any woman who has had a baby knows that the nine months of waiting requires the nth degree of patience, even though you have no choice in the matter.

Perhaps that is precisely why marriage *is* such a spiritual safeguard: in so many instances you simply *have* no choice, and this is fortunate for weak feminine nature. This eliminates waiting for moods to "be holy," or doing only those things which give a smug and satisfying glow. The real difficulty . . . the catch in this testing of the spirit . . . is remembering that the small things do count. In other words, really taking the Sacrament of the Present Moment to heart. I sometimes toy with the idea of tacking up placards around the house—above the sink, en route to the garbage can, over the ironing board—proclaiming: "Offer it up!" "Carry your cross, don't just drag it along behind you!" "All things pass away; patience obtaineth all."

Marriage also deepens a woman's compassion. The mother

in her is much more concerned about starving children in Europe than is the childless person; the wife in her is more disturbed about the housing shortage for young married couples; the neighbor in her is more thoughtful about the sick person in the next block, or the one who needs a baby sitter, or the family that needs hand-me-down clothing.

The general theory, of course, is that the single lay person has more time for good works and personal sanctification than the married woman but . . . does it generally work out that way? I doubt it. Living alone can breed odd and set little ways, selfishness, a turning inward, and perhaps even—with the pious—a certain amount of spiritual pride. After all, the single woman does have more time to join a Third Order, stack up the novenas, be president of the Children of Mary, and work for the Red Cross and the Community Fund.

At this point, St. Jude interrupted me again. *"Psst!"* whispered St. Jude. "Take it easy. Some single people, you know, have no choice in the matter. Where's that compassion you were just talking about? And another thing I'm curious about is this: Don't tell me you just got married in order to work off your temporal punishment?"

"Well, no," said I. "I can't say that was my *primary* reason for marching down the aisle, but the other reasons are so obvious. It would sound like Edgar Guest or a song from Tin Pan Alley."

"Come, come," said St. Jude. "Now don't start getting ornery again. All I want now are a few good points about your own marriage, not just the married state."

"You mean like saying I'm glad my husband is a professor, because I enjoy the university life and because we both share the same interest in books and writing and rejection slips? And because my mother, who bakes beautiful apple pies and is a wizard at sewing, lives with us? And because the children have turned out better looking and smarter than I had any reason to hope for? And because we get to take such nice long vacations in the summer time? And because . . ."

"Precisely," said St. Jude. "And now sum it all up in twenty-five words for that entry in the contest."

I gave a scream. Twenty-five words! And I hadn't yet got around to the really big factor in my marriage—namely, that my husband and I see eye to eye on first things first. For example, neither of us feels that our children are going to curl up and die if they don't have *all* the cultural advantages. (Have you a potential Hollywood starlet in your home? If not, why not? Can your little moppet tap dance, yodel, imitate Mae West, play the electrical guitar, and do the split? If not, why not?) No, we're just mean enough not to care if they *never* get a chance at an M-G-M screen test.

Also, we both agree that frequent weekday Mass and Communion are a mighty good investment. We invest. We also invest (although I sometimes go through the Dark Night of Faith wondering if it's worth the struggle) in the daily Family Rosary.

So, with all this and Heaven too, it wasn't too hard to finish my entry blank for the contest. I had only to add that it was not good for man to live alone . . . that man's basic need was to love and be loved . . . and what did Dorothy Dix have that I didn't have to offer?

Doggone if I didn't, in my dream, win that Nash! True, my entry had run to 2500 succinct words, instead of twenty-five, but the judges were too weary to quibble about a mere technicality. I was so excited that I woke up, sat bolt upright in bed, and started to shake my sleeping mate.

"Hey," I said. "Guess what? St. Jude and I have just won us a new car. Now *you* can take the Plymouth to work and leave me the new Nash. Aren't I wonderful?"

But husbands . . . ! Instead of appreciating all my hard work, he just made a funny little noise that sounded like "glub-umph" and rolled over like a bear settling down for a hard winter.

Oh. well. *c'est la vie. La* married *vie*, anyway.

How to Make a Convert Singlehanded

Now *there's* a title that haunts me. It's got everything a good, self-respecting title should have: briskness, simplicity, the ring of authority.

What if it does sound like the handcraft section of *American Boy*? ("How to make a necktie rack out of a cigar box.") What if it is fairly crawling with heresy? ("Singlehanded, indeed! You've heard of God's grace, Mrs. Hasley?")

I still say I've got a million-dollar title. It just so happens that I don't have an article to go with it (I've never made a convert in my life), but why be stuffy? You don't catch *me* throwing a good title away just because of a mere technicality. Besides, as I say, the whole business haunts me.

As I understand it, there are three ways to make a convert: A. on your knees; B. on a soapbox; C. on account of the example of your own life. I consider this a very narrow and limited field. Methods B (oratory) and C (example) are, for me, not aids but definite hurdles. This leaves me with Method A (prayer).

I have no quarrel with A, understand, except that it is awkward. I find it very awkward to sink to my knees in front of the Merchants' National Bank where my Protestant friend buttonholes me for a little impromptu session of apologetics. ("So why *can't* you come to my church next Sunday to hear the new minister? Don't I, for heaven's sake, come to your Midnight Mass? Suppose you're too good for us, yah?")

This calls for prayerful guidance, all right, but time is of the essence. I must needs resort to Method B (oratory), and this is too bad. No golden-tongued Chrysostom, I. So I use Method B, and then I go home and get out Method A (prayer), hoping that A will cancel the damage of B. Some days you might just as well not get up in the morning.

You can see for yourself what I'm up against. Personally I'm all for adding tear gas, rubber hoses, and jujitsu tactics and see if I have any better luck. Although I've worked like a horse for Mother Church, I've never made a bona fide convert in my life.

I say bona fide because once I did—sorta—lead someone to Rome. I wear no gold stripe upon my sleeve, proclaiming this feat to the world at large, because I *still* don't think it was according to Hoyle. Frankly, I was just standing there, minding my own business, and suddenly—Eureka!—here was this new Mystical Body cell right beside me. It was entirely an amoeba-like type of reproduction and I can't say that I, the amoeba, had to overstrain myself.

When I decided to join the Church, I broke the glad tidings to my Presbyterian family in a very unheroic manner. I simply left a note propped against the sugar bowl on the kitchen table. "Dear Mama," I wrote. "I'm being baptized a Catholic tomorrow. Hope you don't mind. Love, Lucile."

As it turned out, no one did seem to mind (it was my funeral, not theirs) and it was somewhat of a letdown. I had thought that, possibly, baptism by blood was in store for me.

Anyway, after my anticlimactic water baptism, I went my way quietly. Aside from going to Mass on Sunday and eating tuna fish casserole on Friday, I still—on Monday, Tuesday, Wednesday, Thursday, and Saturday—could have passed for a Presbyterian. Never once did I open my mouth about my new religion. Never once did I indicate, by even a quiver, whether I considered myself—in retrospect—a chosen soul or a sucker. I was giving out no testimonials.

Nevertheless, one year later, *I* received a note. It read, succinctly: "Dear Lucile: I, too, am now a Catholic. Love,

Mother." This sounds pretty silly but it's the truth, so help
me. Our family is the strong silent type.

This solitary conversion leads me to the very unnerving
conclusion that the Trappist vow of silence is my best medium.
Perhaps the apostolate I'm best fitted for is just keeping my
mouth shut, but this is a hard saying. I can't take it. Since
those early days of reticence, I've developed this dread disease
called "Apostolic Itch" and, once it gets in the blood stream,
you're sunk.

The symptoms first appeared when I heard some eloquent
cleric say: "The harvest is plentiful, the laborers few," and I,
the Eager Beaver, rushed in to relieve the man shortage. I had
a strong back, weak mind, and no experience, but I got in.
No labor union.

Today, after much labor and no fruition, I'm asking:
"What's wrong?" I even took a postgraduate course in apologetics down at our local Aquinas book shop and passed my
"Sixteen Steps to the Church" examination with flying colors.
With diploma in hand, I faced my outsider friends with re-
newed confidence. All you had to do was find someone who
accepted Christ's Divinity (not necessary, but it eliminated six
of those arduous steps) and then point out the earmarks of the
True Church. Nothing to it. Simple as shooting fish in a bar-
rel. Then if you happened to forget any subsequent answers,
you could always fall back on the clincher: "Well, the True
Church says so and that's *that.*"

The trouble, as I see it, lies entirely with my Protestant
friends. (I am, wisely, leaving the Synagogue friends alone
until I get better at this. Protestants are tough enough.) They
don't cooperate. They're not interested in logic. They ask entirely the wrong questions. Why can't they play fair by saying
—eagerly, logically, docilely: "Do tell us, *please,* the proofs of
the True Church" instead of throwing me off balance?

Instead they come at me like mosquitoes with annoying little
questions like: "Now, what's this about indulgences?" They
want all the trimmings before the cake's even baked. Or else
they'll say, over the bridge table: "How do you reconcile free
will and predestination?" You're supposed to deal the hand,

make the bid, and settle—in one minute flat—a problem that makes even theologians chew their fingernails. I have been advised (at crucial moments like this) to breathe a prayer to the Holy Ghost and then open my mouth and see what happens. The things that *have* happened . . . ah, you'd never believe me.

(At baptism I received the Holy Ghost and His seven gifts: wisdom, understanding, counsel, fortitude, knowledge, piety, and fear of the Lord. This impressive list made me question the validity of my baptism until it was explained that I had *not* received these gifts in full flower. Remind me, will you, to keep watering those seeds?)

Next, I began to cater to my friends. If they didn't relish logic, we would dispense with logic. I threw my Sixteen Steps diploma away and began to bone up on the miscellaneous hodge-podge found in those Question Box Manuals. It contained no logic and, in some instances, no charity. When a Protestant asked a particularly silly question, the clerical answer was just "Certainly not." The simplicity of this delighted me; I could hardly wait to spring it.

Before long—sure enough—someone asked me: "Isn't it true that if you exhume a Catholic after one hundred years and the corpse is still intact, the person is immediately canonized?"

"Certainly not," I said briskly, and sat back in triumph. That settled *that* point, but my friend didn't look too happy. It didn't seem, for some reason or other, to pave the way to more solid doctrine.

"Well," he began, "supposing the body is *not* intact but there's the odor of lilies. Then he's a saint, huh?"

My faith in the question box tactics was ebbing fast, but I tried it once more. "Certainly *not*," said I.

"Well," he persisted, "supposing the body is *not* intact, there is *no* odor of lilies, but a piece of bone . . ."

It was at this stage of my St. Paul apostolate that I decided to make a layman's retreat, and I do mean *retreat*. Why should *I* break into a cold sweat handling everything from hypothetical exhumed bodies to free will and predestination? Why not pass the buck into professional hands? After all, Mother

Church goes to considerable expense and bother in maintaining seminaries.

I'd get my friend to put his trusting little fist in mine and we'd drop in—casual-like—and discuss the Notre Dame-Army game with Father Dooley. Casual-like, we could then leave touchdowns behind us and sidle up to Eternal Verities. So, chuckling over my own cleverness, I invited the fly to walk into the rectory parlor.

"A priest!" cried my friend hoarsely, leaping back like a startled fawn. "Talk to a *priest*?" In vain did I try to soothe his quivering nerves. If I had suggested a tête-à-tête with Pius XII or that he jump into a cauldron of boiling oil, it would have been one and the same thing.

This reaction goaded me into action. In no time flat I wrote, and sold, an article entitled bluntly: "I Like Priests." It was purely my personal opinion, understand, but I thought it might sow a few seeds. Did it? I wouldn't know. The only enthusiastic response I've had has been from the priests themselves.

One cleric has assured me, in my desolation, that I may never know what seeds I've sown until Judgment Day. A cold, remote comfort. I want to make a walking, breathing convert —here and now—and sit back and enjoy my handiwork.

Moreover, I have it coming to me because Protestants have taken a great toll of my physical strength and spiritual reservoirs. Why I continue even to like them, I wouldn't know. Sometimes I ask myself if I even want such logicless, ornery, trouble-making creatures added to the Fold. I do, though, and —with my tougher customers—I am looking forward to the day of compensation, the day of bright revenge. If they ever turn Catholic, they—in turn—will have to put up with other Protestants asking questions. This cheers me up considerably.

I am looking forward to the day when they will be faced with the same exquisite torture I am now enduring. I select, from a wide selection, four of the most venerable forms of Protestant approach. In parentheses, I enclose four wrong answers.

1. "I'm closer to God taking a walk in the woods than I am

in going to church." (You got something there, bub. I'd rather
be a nature-lover than go to your church, too.)

2. "As I see it, all roads lead to Heaven." (Not *all* roads,
chum. The one you're on is pointing south and is paved with
good intentions.)

3. "You know, our church is *almost* like your church."
(Isn't that a coincidence! I noticed that resemblance just last
Wednesday when I was passing by. I think those slate roofs
are awfully nice, don't you?)

4. "Yes, Sir! I'm as tolerant as they come. Why, some of my
best friends are Catholics." (Oh, go soak your head.)

This sort of thing can lead to your own damnation or your
own spiritual growth. Think of the merit stored up for you
as you refrain from dealing a swift upper-cut or, even, dishing
out those wrong answers. The merit is there for the struggle
but, I warn you, it's enervating. By the time *I'm* through
wrestling with temptation, I'm too worn out to handle the
apologetics.

Now *I*, as a prospective convert, wore no one out. I must
say, modestly, that I was that rare and docile outsider that
lazy missionaries dream about. On my own hook, I simply
went to a priest and said, "Okay, let's get going. What's it all
about?" Thenceforward, I was putty—pure putty—in the
hands of the Romans. By the time we reached the third chap-
ter in the catechism, I was dying to sign on the dotted line.
As I recall, I was annoyed that the priest insisted we at least
finish the catechism before rushing to the baptismal font. He
kept trying to tell me that baptism by desire would tide me
over until I hit the water but I couldn't quite believe him. I
started crossing streets carefully and cautiously lest a truck
mow me down before I was properly prepared for Kingdom
Come.

Well (sigh!), I suppose it's too much to expect that *everyone*
be the dream-child convert *I* was, but—isn't it a shame? It
would make the apostolic life so much simpler.

Fortunately for me, the Church does not demand—like the
Easter Duty—that you *have* to make a convert, but I brood
over my failure. Moreover, I don't much like having the

hierarchy rub salt in the wound. Just last week, in the diocesan paper under the bishop's "Weekly Chat", was a little jab that I took very personally. "Dear flock," wrote my bishop, "Catholics, on the whole, are sound asleep. Have *you* a conversion to your credit?"

No, Bishop, I haven't, but bear with me. I'm awake, I'm trying, and I'm hoping. Surely *somewhere* in this world is some indiscriminate creature who will succumb to my lamebrain type of evangelism.

Magazine Mummie

IT ISN'T just on Mother's Day that my conscience rises up and smites me but on the 364 other days of the year too. Mother's Day is just the highlight; the *official* day to twist the knife in the wound.

I open my gifts from my three little ones (carnation perfume—large economy size—from the dime store; a cactus plant potted in the rear end of a china cat; a sack of peanut brittle) with gladsome cries and all the graciousness of the Queen Mother accepting her due homage. Actually, my conscience and I feel like crawling down the nearest manhole.

My innocent little children are too young, as yet, to realize they're stuck with a ne'er-do-well and shiftless mother but *I* know. And as soon as my little ones are old enough to start reading the slick women's magazines *they're* going to know too. On that unhappy day, not all the perfume in Arabia (not to mention the more potent dime store variety) will be equal to the task of making me fragrant and acceptable in their eyes. They're going to ask for a re-deal. They're going to want a Mummie like those horribly energetic and talented Mummies in the big pretty magazines.

But right now, during this temporary Age of Innocence, my children are perfectly satisfied with their maternal ancestor. They ask but little here below and that's exactly what they're getting. Take, for example, my cooking. While not exactly poisonous, it would never elicit any glowing recommendations from Duncan Hines or an ecstatic "oo-la-la" from the chef at the Waldorf-Astoria. Neither (and here is where I fall down badly) is my food designed to ravish the human eye.

The casseroles that I sling on the table are designed to be eaten as quickly and manfully as possible; one feels no inclination to rush out first and fetch in a photographer to capture the fleeting beauty of my escalloped lima beans.

Nor do my tossed salads resemble a lovely sunset over Lake Manitou. Nor do my fruit arrangements on the buffet resemble a Picasso still life. Nor do my hot biscuits (add ½ cup water to prepared mix) nostalgically carry one back to dem ol' plantation days. Nor are my dinner tables anything to make Emily Post stop cold in her tracks, catch her breath in sheer delight, ejaculate a spontaneous "Bravo! Bravo!"

Frankly, the only place where I might wring out a "Bravo!" would be in a lumber camp. Plain clean grub . . . that's my forte . . . and all reduced to the lowest common denominator in terms of effort, artistry, and time expended. Life's too short for all these fancy trimmings and I cast my lot with Chesterton as he appraises, with a fine detachment, the nuisance of being civilized!

"He (man) gets inside a tower of clothing, a tower of wool and flax. His hair he beats angrily with a bristly tool. For this is the Law. Downstairs, a more monstrous ceremony awaits him. He has to put things inside of himself. He does, being naturally polite. Nor can it be denied that a weird satisfaction follows. . . ."

That is my point, precisely. *If* a weird satisfaction follows, I claim the food is a success. No need to have it look all primed for an Atlantic City beauty contest.

My family, of course, is conditioned to my repulsive-looking food by now but strangers sometimes leap back in dismay. So, whenever I want my dinner parties to be a real success, I blindfold my guests. This device is *so* much simpler than slaving over a hot stove all afternoon that I wonder why the women's magazines haven't caught on to it? In addition, it adds a touch of intrigue to the occasion to have one's blindfolded guests morbidly speculating as to what in thunder

they're eating. On really festive occasions, we give prizes for
the best guesses.

Now, idyllic as this arrangement is, I have to admit that the
blindfold device is frowned upon in the better circles. I am
perfectly aware that food *should* be so lovingly and artis-
tically prepared that the mere sight of it, thirty yards off,
automatically titillates the taste buds and starts the flow of
saliva down to mingle with the gastric juices. I am, as I say,
perfectly aware of this theory but in much the same way as
I am aware of Einstein's theory of relativity. It has no practical bearing on my daily routine.

The taste buds and saliva of my children conveniently start
operating with little or no provocation. We even have to spell
out items like "p-e-a-n-u-t b-u-t-t-e-r" to keep the baby from
getting out of control. So, if a plain peanut butter sandwich
will automatically throw the switch, why beat my brains out
trying to make it a *beautiful* peanut butter sandwich? And if
my children drool at the sight of an unsightly batch of jello
(imitation cherry with a tin of fruit cocktail dumped in), why
should I overstrain myself? Why let them even know that
other mothers make individual molded gelatine desserts; wondrous in architectural structure, quivering technicolor beau-
ties that would do credit to a Walt Disney fantasy.

At any rate, I now (thanks to my careful cunning) have a
delightfully hoodwinked family to cook for. Anything more
exotic than vanilla absolutely frightens them: they recoil from
the unknown. Occasionally this proves embarrassing (such
as a child spewing forth, in public, a piece of almond cake or
rum-flavored sauce) but, on the whole, it has paid dividends.
It has hurt my conscience, true, but I have netted untold
hours of leisure. AND, my children are under the impression
that my performance as a cook is not only satisfactory but
standard!

Obviously, a house founded upon shifting sands is a doomed
domicile. One of these fine days my children are going to pick
up a woman's magazine, get a technicolor load of the kind of
food other people eat, and demand an accounting. Grape-
fruits cut out like baskets and filled with deep sea delicacies;

real violets and lilies-of-the-valley stuck into the cake frosting; intricately twisted bread sticks; watermelon balls; radishes carved like rosebuds; stuffed, braided and curled celery stalks; cucumber wheels; tinted pears . . .

Then (and oh, I can see it so plainly) "children's faces looking up, holding wonder like a cup" as they say: "Mama! What are all those pretty things?"

And I, hanging my head, will have to admit that it is FOOD. And oh, the ignominy of having my children point to something as commonplace as a baked potato and not recognize it. "What's that thing, Mama?" they'll say, and I'll have to say: "A baked potato, darling," and then they'll say: "But, Mama, *our* baked potatoes don't look like that."

The whole sordid tale will then have to be told. Portia will have to face life. I'll have to admit that *other* mothers oil and massage the potato skins, mash and restuff the potato, garnish with melted cheese, chipped beef, paprika, chicory, escarole, romaine, chives, watercress, and shredded eggplant and then —oh, brave new world—stick an American flag in the middle of the whole affair. (This, of course, is for the fourth of July. Labor Day, Pentecost, the battle of Bunker Hill, the sinking of the Merrimac, and other historic occasions call for their own appropriate motifs. All magazine mummies are not only extremely ingenious in this regard but keep a scrupulous eye on the calendar for likely holidays. I, crude peasant that I am, simply observe fish on Fridays.)

But are you beginning to see what I mean? After one squint at that sublimated and citizenship-conscious potato, do you think my children are going to settle for just an ole baked Idaho with a hunk of margarine slapped aloft? Not even an Old Glory holding down the fort?

Believe me, the women's magazines are fraught with danger. Why, even the straight ads are dynamite. Sheer dynamite. If my children started reading, and believing, these ads, my present control would be shattered.

"Mummie!" they would shout joyously as they troop into the living room. (All children in ads call their mothers "Mummie" for some repulsive reason.) "Mummie," they would shout, "we just tracked a lot of mud on your freshly scrubbed floor but it doesn't matter, does it, Mummie? Because your floor is always glo-coated."

Laughing in gay amusement (instead of beating them over the head as of yore), I would have to respond: "Oh, that's perfectly all right, pets. Mummie was all dressed for the faculty tea this afternoon, but think nothing of it. Mummie will enjoy getting down on her knees and wiping up the mud with just cold water, in one simple easy operation, because I'll get a chance to see how my floor retains its original lustre. Thank you, my darlings."

Glory be, my children are still too absorbed in their own reading material (The Bobbsey Twins at the Seashore, The Bobbsey Twins in the Rockies, The Bobbsey Twins in the Swamp, The Bobbsey Twins at Sing Sing, etc.) to pay any attention to mine. *But,* I'm on my guard. My exposure is inevitable, of course, but I'm not voluntarily going to give myself up. I'm hiding these magazines that would—with one horrendous blast—expose this fugitive as something less than the angels, something less than a Magazine Mummie.

The Alien Corn

MY FAVORITE sport, on rainy afternoons, is to get out my typewriter and pretend I'm Moses. It *was* Moses, wasn't it, who led his people into the Promised Land? Or do I mean Elijah? Anyway, it makes no difference. The plight of my people, my fellow Catholic converts, is so desperate that they can't afford to be choosey. Moses, Elijah, Mrs. Hasley . . . they can use *anyone*.

Yet, oddly enough, this self-appointed role as Moses is a thankless one. Difficult, too. Since a conversion to the true Faith is not, precisely, a matter for condolences, I find that many people have a closed mind toward the convert's dilemma. Some Catholic citizen is always sure to complain: "But *I've* never seen a desperate convert."

Well, naturally not. Not, at least, with the naked eye. Converts lead lives of *quiet* desperation; they don't go around making a big hullabaloo about it. Besides which, I have actually met converts who didn't even *know* they were desperate until I called it to their attention. Some of them thank me, some of them don't, but . . . he who hath ears, let him hear.

The truth of the matter is that converts are a lost and neglected tribe: a tribe that wanders, lonely as a cloud, amid the alien corn. I'm not raising funds, urging CARE packages for converts, or trying to get them into Palestine but I *am* concerned about their infiltration. Many converts, after Baptism, remain half-breeds—half Catholic, half Protestant—and lead a spiritual hand to mouth existence that would break your heart.

May I go ahead and break your heart? (I can see right now that you don't believe any of this but wait until I expound.) At the top of the heap you have converts like Sigrid Undset, Jacques and Raissa Maritain, Christopher Dawson, Evelyn Waugh, and a host of other stars in the firmament. These converts are not, exactly, drooping and wilting in their corners; they are not, exactly, waiting for either me or Moses to lead them on. (In this topflight category, of course, I automatically include all of Msgr. Fulton Sheen's converts. When he gets through instructing *his* people, they're ready for a lecture tour.)

At the bottom of the heap, you have converts—perhaps out on the Fiji Islands—who will never grasp anything beyond the Four Last Things. They don't need Moses, either.

The converts *I'm* yearning over are the average citizens in the great in-between: the ones left to wander, amid the alien corn, with only the Baltimore Catechism as a guide book. Now, the catechism is fine (I give it my imprimatur, especially the revised edition that states Heaven is not restricted to Catholics) but it doesn't offer much in the line of practical cheer or useful household hints. It doesn't help the convert to shake that strange Ellis Island feeling, that "I yust come over in the beeg ship" complex.

Take little Mrs. Liftnagle out in Akron, Ohio: a late refugee from the First Methodist Church. Mrs. Liftnagle, with only six weeks' instruction tucked behind her, doesn't know Gregorian chant from a Perry Como disk or a ferial day from a ferris wheel. She has but recently, to tell you the truth, discovered that two candles on the altar forecast a low Mass coming up.

Here's where I come in. Do I tell Mrs. Liftnagle all about Gregorian chant or a ferial day? Hardly. (No one has told *me* yet.) What *I* do is warmly congratulate her, from the bottom of my heart, on the two candles. That's good, I tell her, very good. She's making great liturgical strides.

In the realm of theology, I am equally helpful. Mrs. Liftnagle, with only the Apostles' Creed to lean on, isn't quite up to the rare and purified approach of Aquinas but she can understand *my* jargon.

My mixed-breed jargon, plus my fifth grade level of Christian Doctrine, plus my unerring instinct for learning things the hard way, make me—sans peer!—the Convert's Delight. Not the Vatican's Delight, let me make clear, but the delight of converts who need a spot of comfort.

Converts are delighted, tickled to death, to find someone else as theologically retarded and as clumsy on their knees as they are. I bring happiness and relief into countless homes simply by exposing, in cold print, the depths of my ignorance and . . . not feeling too cut up over those depths! I don't feel too badly because I'm having a fine time, haven't once been excommunicated, and have a Theory to bolster me up.

My Theory is that anyone who says he has the Alpha and Omega of Catholicism down *cold* is either a dolt, a liar, or a mental case laboring under delusions of grandeur. Even the great Aquinas, shortly before his death, exclaimed (in reference to his unfinished *Summa*): "What rubbish it is! Mihi videtur ut palia." (I can't translate that but it doesn't *sound* good, does it?)

Consider further. The average Catholic receives eight to sixteen years of Catholic instruction, while the seminarians sweat it out for an even longer stint. So, converts, lift up your heads. God, they tell me, is quite reasonable in his demands. And the really nice part (the silver lining) is that you'll never have to resort to collecting antique pickle forks or blown glass figurines or match folders for a hobby. Trying to catch up with Mother Church affords an exciting and challenging project that will keep you well occupied for the rest of your days. Belloc says: "If you want to have a very adventurous life, be a thorough Catholic," but *I* say it's plenty adventurous even for a half-baked beginner.

While it is true that I can, by now, make the Sign of the Cross with all the careless swish of an old timer, it is only a small step forward. After years in the Faith, I can still ask more questions than Dr. I. Q. with a lady in the balcony. Even on my death bed, receiving Extreme Unction, I will probably rear up and say: "Now, wait a minute, let's get this straight. Am I holding the candle right? (And are you sure it's blessed and made of pure beeswax?) How's my disposition? What're you going to do with that cotton? What does the oil mean? Am I getting all the indulgences I have coming to me? Would you mind cutting out the Latin and repeating that last sentence in basic English, please?"

The priest *may* end up wishing for death himself. What price peace?

It's perfectly possible, of course, that I may run across an illuminating article on Extreme Unction some day and be able to give that bedside priest some good pointers. Things keep opening up all the time and never a month goes by that I don't stumble across something new and stimulating. Last month it was the "Heroic Act of Charity."

Amazed and dazzled by this new discovery, I rushed forth to amaze and dazzle my friends. Who, thought I, *could* be so heroic as voluntarily to take a chance on being the last man out of Purgatory? Yet the first born Catholic I tried to impress with my heroic tidings stopped me with a casual, "Oh, sure, I made the Heroic Act back in the eighth grade."

This is the sort of treatment I get all the time. Every little gem of Catholic lore that I proudly display is brushed rudely aside by people who have known it all their lives and don't want to hear any more about it, thanks. How can I possibly compete with people who started imbibing Catholicism along with their Pablum? How can I possibly come up with any hot theological scoops?

Perhaps this is the real reason (not just my tender brooding heart) that makes me concentrate on new converts. One jump ahead of them, I get a chance to show off. Shucks, I'll bet a new convert wouldn't know the Heroic Act from the Marshall Plan.

Lest anyone wonder how all this could possibly cheer up converts, let me explain that my own quaint method of dispensing cheer is via the misery method. Misery loves company, I always say, even though the "misery" is only the creaking and groaning that goes with adjusting Protestant knee-joints to a Catholic prie-dieu.

To accept, with joy, the basic verities is one thing. To think, act, smell, talk, and feel like a Roman Catholic is quite another. I am personally convinced that if all the blood, sweat, and tears involved were—collectively—offered up, Russia could be converted in twenty-four hours.

But for those converts who are more concerned about themselves than about Russia, I do have a word of genuine cheer. It takes years before you can wend your way through all this alien corn with any degree of grace and certainty. You don't become a full-fledged Catholic overnight; it has to seep gradually into your bones and blood stream. And whereas your funny questions and doubts may show that you still have mixed blood in your veins, it also shows that the blood is still circulating. Some of the born Catholics act as if *their* blood vessels, especially those leading to the cranium, were clamped off with tourniquets. Of what value to have pure blue blood in your veins if it isn't reaching the mind or heart?

It is perfectly possible, you understand, to be dumb *and* holy but there's nothing in Canon Law that insists on this combination. Having brains, and using them, won't ever keep you from being canonized. Neither does the Church officially proclaim that converts automatically receive Infused Theology at the baptismal font. Yet, unfortunately for the converts, there is a beautiful bit of folk lore . . . that's been handed down from generation to generation . . . that is almost as fantastic. This is the legend that converts-always-know-more-about-their-religion-than-the-born-Catholics. How this vicious rumor ever started, God only knows. Maybe Luther. All I know is that I'm willing to believe in pixies and I'm willing to believe the moon is made of green cheese but *here* I draw the line. A little gay whimsy in this prosaic world of ours is all right but this, *this* is carrying things too far.

Yet even those Catholics who clearly perceive a dumb and desperate convert when they meet one remain strangely placid about the situation. They don't actually quibble about the convert's right to the Promised Land, the inner sanctum circle,

but how many *help*? This is what burns me up to a fine crisp.
What wonderful apostles these converts (bursting with fresh
interest, zeal, gratitude) would be if only their education
weren't cut short.

There are books and lectures, yes. There are study clubs,
yes. There are spiritual directors, yes. But the greenhorn convert needs a guide to lead him *to* the guides. They aren't
just hanging around on street corners.

Catholics move heaven and earth to train their young—all
hope lies with the coming generation!!!—but the adult converts are polished off in no time flat. If adults are worth
baptizing, aren't they worth a follow-up? (Even the Hoover
Vacuum Sweeper company solicitously sends out a man every
six months to check the parts.)

The question may be raised: *are* adults worth baptizing?
Personally, I feel that this is not too rash an assumption.
Christ, if I recall correctly, said to his apostles: "Follow me."
Not: "How old will you be on your next birthday and have
you had a medical check-up recently?" Come to think about
it, only St. John was a stripling youth among that early band.
Even Aquinas (and don't believe him when he calls his stuff
"rubbish") claims that we will all be around thirty-three
years old in Heaven. He talks as if thirty-three, not eighteen,
is rather a decent—even a heavenly—age for one's Eternity.

But as a sop to the Youth Movement, may I gently ask who
is to produce and rear your Catholic Actionists if not the
adults? With more than 330,000 U. S. A. converts in the past
three years, maybe the Church shouldn't overlook their im-
portance as mamas and papas. The mamas and papas set the
pace. You want more half-breeds, maybe?

Also, strangely enough, converts are great convert-makers.
Not that they necessarily know what they're talking about
but . . . well, they've got that sympathetic touch, see? They,
too, in Sunday School used to sing "Jesus Wants Me For A
Sunbeam" and "Brighten The Corner Where You Are" and
these nostalgic connections form a firm base for higher apologetics. Of course, if the converts only knew what they were
talking about the apologetics could be a little higher.

I would also like to point out (even though I'm beginning to feel like a bird dog by now) that, in Catholic writing, it's the converts who overrun the field. This would almost seem to indicate that the convert, like the goose that laid the golden egg, is worth fattening and grooming . . . to safeguard the interests of Mother Church, if nothing else.

The Church should squarely face the fact that every convert who can push a pencil around is going to break into print, sooner or later, to defend the Faith and restore all things in Christ. Like death and taxes, nothing can be done about this. It's just something to be faced with fortitude.

Obviously, this yen to edify the world is a case of fools rushing in where angels fear to tread, but if the angels are just going to sit back and let the fools take over, they have only themselves to blame.

Loopholes

THE evening is young, the evening is promising, and—
suddenly—the axe falls. The priest you've invited over to the
house (as the *pièce de résistance* for the evening's gathering)
gets to his feet with seeming reluctance. "Sorry to break this
up, folks," says he, "but I'll have to be getting along. Haven't
said my Office yet."

The first time this happened, I was all holy and breathless
concern. I rushed around hunting for his hat, earnestly assur-
ing him that I understood perfectly, and practically pushed
him out on the sidewalk. You wouldn't catch *me* interfering
with anyone's prayer-life.

The next time this happened, it was still all right. But the
next time I said to myself: "Look. This is getting monotonous.
This is a clerical loophole, pure and simple." That unsaid
breviary, I decided, was a mighty handy gadget: the perfect
passport to hand one's hostess.

Now I don't begrudge priests this little liturgical exit of
theirs (it merely shatters the evening), but I'd like to tip off
my fellow laymen. *We* have a magic formula for an exit, too.
The next time you're asked to perform some Herculean parish
job, just say to your priest: "I'm sorry, Father, but I just
can't. I'd have to neglect my state of life and that comes first,
doesn't it?"

Believe me, those are conquering words, for we work out
our salvation—says Mother Church—performing the duties
of our state of life. Used as a gag to get out of something, this

state of life argument is practically watertight because no one, save One, can peer behind scenes and check up on you. Used as a genuine excuse, you have all the cherubim and seraphim solidly behind you.

Any way you look at it, it's a convenient bit of theology to have on hand—a shield of good purpose—and you're more than welcome to the tip. Myself, I can't use it. Me, I need a different brand of tactics to defend myself.

For instance, a female acquaintance drops in for an unexpected visit. The living room is chaos and there in the middle of chaos am I—calmly writing, say, an essay entitled "Loopholes."

"With three children," says my visitor, "*how* do you find time to write?" (All she needs is to look around but she asks it anyway. Her voice is heavy with implications.)

"By neglecting my state of life," I say promptly and agreeably. This is known as the grabbing-the-bull-by-the-horns maneuver. My visitor can only swallow hard and content herself with furtive glances around for cobwebs; dark mental conjectures as to whether or not the beds are made upstairs.

Next, I bring out my quotations. "It takes a heap o' living to make a house a home," I say unctuously, gazing around at all the heaps o' living. If this doesn't seem to go over, I abandon Edgar Guest for Father Dowling of Cana Conference fame. "Better a dirty living room," I quote airily, "than dirty nerves." And, as a final desperate measure, I can always go Biblical: "Martha, Martha, thou art busy with many things; Mary hath chosen the better part." (Putting myself in the role of Mary is really desperate.)

I've got lots of other quotations up my sleeve, too, but it's obvious that the lady doth protest too much. The lady doth know she's on the defensive.

I've done a lot of research looking for loopholes (Loophole Lucile, they call me) in my role as housewife. Conclusion: No loopholes. Anything edifying that I may now say on the subject should rightly be in quotes, for it's not my idea. It's what *they* keep telling me, as they turn me around and head me toward the kitchen sink again.

"But I don't like to do housework," I wail. "I'm not any good at it." (Let no male, at this point, wag his finger in condemnation. There is nothing in the blood stream of the newly-born female that guarantees, *ipso facto,* that she's going to delight in fine stitches, swapping recipes, and dusting Venetian blinds. Moreover, what if—after the marriage ceremony —all men were automatically expected to become lawyers. Would they all make *good* lawyers?)

One clerical answer, cheerless but lofty, is: "Do it anyway. Consider it as a challenge!"

Challenge is the word, all right, for if ever anyone was born all thumbs as regards the housewifely arts, I'm your lady. Still, that word does seem to bring out the Joan of Arc in me. "Challenge!" I cry aloud as—simultaneously—the phone rings, the applesauce bubbles over on the stove, and the gas man pounds on the back door. Blessed Martin was a lucky soul with his gift of bilocation.

Another clerical answer is: "Offer up all suffering for the love of God." I gaze at my two weeks' collection of ironing and mutter to myself, "For the love of God!" I sometimes wonder, though, if I give it the correct liturgical emphasis.

You can see for yourself that my attitude leaves much to be desired, but there's this about it. Some women, according to folklore, positively revel in housework. They look forward to spring house cleaning as a debutante looks forward to the local charity ball. Small credit to them, say I, but a jewel-studded crown for the woman who grits her teeth and does it anyway. One extra jewel added if you *don't* grit your teeth.

My main grievance against the duties of the home is the fleeting, the transitory, character of one's labor. Dutifully and even cheerfully, I may scour the house from top to bottom. It's even a *good* feeling. Pleasantly tired, I sink into a chair and survey my gleaming castle with a "well-done, my good and faithful servant" complacency. This is where the word *transitory* comes in. Four hours later the place looks as if the Russian army had marched through.

I bake a pie. It has only taken me the better part of the day—*The Boston Cook Book* in hand—but it's a beauty. I'm so proud of it that I want to place it on the mantel, call the neighbors in, and let everyone admire—in hushed silence— my handiwork. This is not the way it works out. The first thing I know the family is wiping crumbs off faces, grossly, and I'm right back where I started.

There are moments when I think that if my salvation rests on the cheerfulness and alacrity with which I surmount all this, God rest my soul. Truly, I've given this state of life problem a good deal of thought and a thorough study of it is like reading all the fine print on the back of an insurance policy: more clauses, more technicalities, more hemming in.

Let us consider, in detached and scholarly fashion, this fine print. I understand that originally the word "wife" meant "weaver." Passing over this with a brief shudder, I come to our twentieth century label of "housewife." Now who, to tear the word apart, wants to be a wife to a house? It's as bad as the weaving and it seems to me that the Holy Sacrament of Matrimony warrants a more inspiring banner to march behind. In poetry women are hailed as "empire-builders," "molders of men," "faces that launch ships," "hands that rock cradles," but we are invariably listed as—ugh!—housewives on all official records. I like the woman who, fed up with this classification, wrote on a census report: "Occupation: Typhoid carrier."

Anyway, let us consider the little weaver/housewife/typhoid carrier. Suppose, after getting married, she discovers that housework for her is simply a tote-that-barge, lift-that-pail arrangement. She even tries it as a challenge and the challenge falls flat on its face. Can she then, without fear of excommunication, hire a housekeeper to pick up the challenge? Sure. This is the beautiful gossamer dream that has kept me going for years. What more pleasant, I ask you, than to sit back and supervise someone *else's* state of life? The only flaw is (1) find housekeeper and (2) be able to support her. My one lovely loophole that is morally approved comes, woe is me, equipped with a Yale padlock.

Let us now go from padlocks to pitfalls. With the greatest of ease women can stumble into two other dangers: over-

play or underplay their state of life with a vengeance. Don't
think for a moment that Mrs. Loophole is the only one who
has to watch her step. Mrs. Loophole has friends:

Mrs. Underplay is not necessarily a caricature of the escapist
mother—one foot on the bar rail in some swishy Reno
night club. She might well be that militant Catholic lady in
the next block—one foot in every committee in town. Is she
efficient? Look at the record! If all the rummage sales, bingo
parties, bazaars, and lottery projects that she has engineered
were laid end to end . . . ah, but mere statistics cannot do her
justice. You not only see her Good Works but you can hear
them a mile away. After all, sounding brass and tinkling
cymbals make quite a racket.

She's in the front line of battle, straining for a Laetare
Medal, but . . . well, have you ever seen her husband? He's
that rather seedy-looking gent with the hunted look in his
eyes. The housework and child-rearing, singlehanded, are beginning to tell on him. He wasn't cut out to be a mother.

Mrs. Overplay, *au contraire*, revels and rejoices in her
role as door mat for the family. You can't miss seeing the
carefully adjusted halo because she, herself, keeps it as polished
as her front parlor. She it is who says, tight-lipped, "Charity
begins at home." And her life project is to see that not one
drop of charity, falling as the gentle rain from heaven,
descends on anyone not a blood relative. When she prays the
Our Father it is strictly a closed family affair with Mama,
Daddy, Darlene, and little Ralphie as sole beneficiaries.

State of life, as you can see, has tricky undercurrents and it
takes considerable talent to be a Mrs. Evenplay. You have to
learn when to strike out boldly, when to tread water, and
when to hit back for shore. Mrs. Evenplay, rare creature, takes
Catholic Action seriously (she even reads the Pope's encycli-
cals!!) but she doesn't feel that Christianity will collapse un-
less she, personally, heads every committee. She doesn't let
the Home Action get lost in the shuffle.

Just like the next person, she sometimes feels flattened out
by the unheroic character of her days, but she has a private
little picker-upper. Once she read: "Pick up a pin for the love

of God and perhaps you can save a soul." Mrs. Evenplay takes
this fantastic statement seriously because the Little Flower
—who made a specialty of just picking up pins—proved her
point.

On this solitary note of edification, I bid farewell to my
foursome: Mrs. Loophole, Mrs. Underplay, Mrs. Overplay and
Mrs. Evenplay. Actually, they're four very nice Christian ladies.
Three of them, though, could use a little overhauling.

Nightmare of an Apostle

THE strain is beginning to tell on me. I am fast developing a split personality—thanks to the Holy Roman Catholic and Apostolic Church—and I sometimes fear for my last estate. I don't begrudge Mother Church my services, understand, but what's to become of my poor little personality? Since I never had much to begin with, I can scarcely afford to have it split up on me.

The whole trouble, of course, is that I am trying to be all things to all men and, whereas St. Paul could get away with it, *I* find it a definite strain. My Jekyll-Hyde role in the realm of amateur apologetics finds me doling out arsenic with one hand and sweetness and light with the other. It's interesting work, of course, but it means living dangerously. It also causes nightmares.

The arsenic, naturally, is for the lame-brain Catholics who are gumming up the works, the lame-brains who need a good strong dash of the fear of the Lord. The sweetness and light, in the other hand, is for the little lambs who have either just entered the fold or are looking the place over. Now, offhand, maybe this sleight-of-hand looks simple but it certainly isn't for *me*. It calls for prudence, and prudence isn't something you can just pick up at the corner drug store.

For one thing, the lame-brains are to be given *just* enough arsenic to make them get a wiggle on but not enough to kill them off. The Church frowns on manslaughter. This is not too terribly hard to bear in mind but it's the questing lambs who present the real problem. The lambs—at least in the first tender stages of their searching for the Light—need a certain amount of sheltering from the raw winds.

Am I luring the lambs in with underhanded methods? No. Only, in selling the Church, I would first like to point out the tabernacle, the confessional, and the prie-dieu before mentioning that the roof could use a little repair work.

The lambs will, sooner or later, have to be taught the facts of life (controversy within, persecution without, plus a goodly sprinkling of unworthy stewards, money-changers, sleeping apostles, and what-have-you) *but* they should first be given a fair chance to *reach* the Light.

They deserve a chance to get a spiritual head start. They should not be prematurely and rudely overwhelmed by the wounds in the Mystical Body before getting a good square look at the healthy and indestructible side.

It's a neat little problem. I don't advocate throttling the reformers, because I'm on the side of the reformers. All I'm saying is that, at the same time, it hurts my business. My business, as a convert, is to say: "Come on in, the water's fine."

So, what's the answer? I dunno. (St. Paul would never say "I dunno" but what better can you expect from a split personality?) All I know is that this being an apostle calls for a clear head, a steady hand, and a delicate touch. Sometimes, alack, I have the delicate touch of the Village Blacksmith. I have even been told that I sound as if I were riding against the Turks, shouting: "All for God and St. Wenceslaus!"

Still, that isn't my chief worry. Let the Turks worry. No, I think all might go well if I only keep my wits about me, but my recurrent nightmare is that some day I'm going to get mixed up. I'm going to forget which hand is which and hand out the wrong dose to the wrong person. Sweetness and light won't damage anyone, but the arsenic . . . ah, I would have a fine time explaining to the coroner just exactly what happened.

"I meant to give my little lamb a copy of *Faith of Our Fathers*," I would sob, "but I accidentally grabbed up a copy of *Integrity* instead. It caused convulsion, spasm, shock, and . . . well, he just never regained consciousness. I didn't mean to do it, honest."

After the coroner releases me on bail, I'll have to go around and make my peace with *Integrity*. Along with all my other troubles, heaven knows that I won't want a law suit on my hands. No, not even in a nightmare.

"*Integrity*," I will say, sinking to one knee, "I love you dearly. Believe me. I read you from cover to cover, I riddle you like a termite, but you *do* see what I mean, don't you? That poor little lamb had just got through his Baltimore Catechism . . . where all was calm, all was serene . . . and then you hit him like the Great Gale of 1873. I didn't even have a chance to yell at him to hold onto his hat."

"Well, *Integrity*," I will continue, in a wheedling voice, "you see my point? You do a powerful lot of good for the old guard, the inner circle, but you're an awful shock to the tenderfoot. Heaven preserve us, that wee lamb never even *dreamed* that there was all this inner strife and turmoil and controversy within the Church. It was a blow, *Integrity*, a mortal blow, but I don't blame you. *I* was the one that slipped up. *I* handed him the lethal dose. Let's call the law suit off, eh?"

After making my peace with *Integrity*, I will then (trouble, trouble, naught but trouble) probably have to go see the parish priest.

"It wasn't your fault, Father," I will say. "Your instructions were solid . . . and I realize you can't cover *everything* . . . but I do have a suggestion. How's about giving your converts, at the baptismal font, a copy of . . . well, say, Suhard's *The Church: Growth or Decline?* It will not only give them a clear picture of the Church today but serve as a bracer. In time, they will then be ready to read *Integrity* with profit instead of just keeling over cold."

After I have made my peace with the pastor, I will wearily trudge home to my typewriter. I've been a busy bee; I am indeed weary; but there is still work to be done. I now must write an epistle to the Corinthians . . . or whatever tribe best corresponds to my fellow laymen.

"Dear Corinthians," I will write. "That little lamb is dead
but for whom doth the bell toll? Brothers, it tolls for thee . . .
it tolls for me. A perfectly good Mystical Body cell has perished
on the vine. Listen, you Corinthians, what did *you* . . ."

Well, lucky for the Corinthians, the heavy tolling of the
bells in this nightmare always wakes me up at this point. The
Corinthians are spared an epistle that would singe their eyebrows. In a way, it's a shame because—while it might not do
the Corinthians any good—I think *I'd* feel much better to get
it off my chest. Amongst the Corinthians are a few professional
crapehangers that I would like to shoot on sight, without even
waiting for the whites of their eyes.

How is the state of the Church in Russia? France? Lower
Slobbovia? Illinois? Podunk Center?

The crapehangers know. They know everything. They know
everything, that is, except that they're running only on two
cylinders. Hope has been scratched. As I harken to their dirges
(background music of *Danse Macabre*) I feel a mighty im-
pulse to drown them out by spouting Péguy:

"Faith is a church, a cathedral rooted in the soil of France.
Charity is a hospital, an almshouse which gathers up all the
    miseries of the world.
But if it weren't for hope, all that would be nothing but a
    cemetery."

It seems to me that these crapehangers are following an
empty hearse to the cemetery. How can you conduct the last
rites without a corpse? It isn't liturgical.

If I were to take these dirges to heart, I would indeed feel
that I—as an ex-Protestant—had been sold down the river.
Old Sucker Hasley. Sucked in by a man who, nearly 2000
years ago, said: "Thou art Peter and upon this rock I will
build my church; and the gates of Hell shall not prevail
against it."

If one can't believe in Christ's own promise, one can well
afford to weep. And yet some of these Corinthians seem to
get so little out of the Church, personally, that their tears
just don't make sense. What difference if the Church expires?

I should think, from listening to them, that it would be a case of good riddance. No, I honestly don't follow them. They truly sound as if their Faith wasn't a gift but a mill-stone around their necks.

Maybe they don't realize how it sounds but, especially to an outsider, there seems to be this strong undertone: "Yes, God help me, I'm a Catholic. Lift that load, tote that barge. Come, let us all line up . . . single file . . . at the Wailing Wall. Life ain't no crystal staircase, son."

Okay. Life ain't no crystal staircase, son. But I would like to ask this crucified Corinthian just one question.

"If the Church is such an unmitigated mess, would you . . . with a clear conscience . . . still want your best friend to become a Catholic? You *would?* Honest? Well, then, why not give your poor friend some little inkling that Catholicism has a few compensations? No outsider, in his right mind, would join a Church that was falling apart at the seams; that offered *nothing* but grief and strife and limitations and lamentations."

Oh, I know the comeback to this. "Only a fool would fiddle out a sweetness-and-light aria while Rome is burning." And yet, the three young men in the Fiery Furnace sang canticles; David, before battles, whipped out his lyre; and St. Francis couldn't help bursting out with occasional vocal numbers. I don't think the *Danse Macabre* was in his repertoire, either.

Well, maybe it was all a lot of foolishness but they *did* bear witness to their joy in Christ. "If you want to become a canonized saint," says Father Vann, "you must first become a notoriously happy person." Could be that I do these crape-hangers a grave injustice. Maybe they *are* deliriously happy that they're Catholics but, from where I'm sitting, I see some mighty sour faces. And if I were still a Presbyterian, they wouldn't tempt *me* to join their ranks.

The Mona Lisas

Not so very long ago I innocently wrote an article entitled "I Like Priests," based on the simple thesis that priests —as people—had considerably brightened my life.

Well, no one cared whether my life had been brightened or not, but a lot of people seemed stirred by my thought-provoking theory that priests *are* people. As a result of this brilliant and daring hypothesis, I now find myself one of the busiest anthropologists of the day. I barely have time to get my housework done. They keep wanting me to track down and identify all sorts of peculiar creatures.

Let me say right here that amateur anthropology is no bed of roses. Especially if you tackle it as I do. My blunt statement that "priests are my favorite people" was equivalent to climbing out on the limb of a tree and sawing it off behind me. Reproachful cries immediately rent the air. Didn't I like *nuns?* Hadn't *they* brightened my life, too?

This chip-on-shoulder attitude frightens me. If I wrote that yes, I did *so* like nuns, then someone else would say: "What's the matter? Don't you like the Young Christian Workers?" I can foresee an endless, desperate series: "I Like Laymen . . ." "I Like the Pope" . . . "I Like the Daughters of Isabella . . ."

The truth of the matter is that I know as much about nuns as I do about tropical fish. (Another future article: "I Like Tropical Fish.") Being an adult convert, I was not exposed to a parochial education under nuns and, hence, they have neither brightened nor dimmed my life. Nuns and I have passed each other like ships in the dark and I haven't the faintest idea as to what *really* goes on under those white fluted halos and flowing black veils. To me, nuns are just so many walking and breathing Mona Lisas. You know the Mona Lisa: the folded hands, the serene brow, the guess-what's-behind-my-smile.

Now if there's anything to whet the interest of an anthropologist, it's a Mona Lisa. Especially when you know Mona was once plain Susie Smith, as feminine and ornery as they come. Intensive research might bring to light just what happened to Susie and what's still happening to Susie, but, frankly, the assignment scares me. If generations of anthropologists haven't yet figured out what makes the ordinary woman tick, how fathom a nun? Who knows the wind? Who knows a female religious?

I do have, however, one avenue of approach. I am prepared to speak, with no guesswork, on the fortitude of nuns under two acid conditions: (1) in the dentist's chair and (2) in the infirmary. Ingrid Bergman, as a movie nun, *has* had T.B. but—to the best of my knowledge—she hasn't yet had her teeth drilled. I believe this to be a new and valuable sidelight.

It just so happens that my female dentist is a Third Order Dominican who caters to nuns. (How I, a mere layman, managed to squeeze into her holy clientele is a mystery, but I suspect she uses me as a dental guinea pig.) Anyway, neither the dentist *nor* her nuns are exactly brightening my life.

For one thing, my dental appointments are always being switched or cancelled at the last minute because some Sister Gabriel's tooth is presumably hurting worse than mine. For another thing, even after I am enthroned in the dentist's chair, my position is still precarious, still that of the underdog. A tooth is excavated, my mouth piled full of cotton wads, my jaws propped open with steel braces: I am all ready for the filling. This is the signal for some nun from out of town to drop in for a social call on my dentist. I—abandoned on the torture rack—can hear them outside the door, falling upon each other with glad yips of joy. By the time they are through visiting, my jaw is permanently dislocated.

Another thing I resent (I told you before I liked *priests*) is the way nuns keep cool. How, on a sweltering day, can they sit there in the reception room calmly flipping pages of *Dental Hygiene*, calmly looking like so many penguins on a block of ice? *I* have on a sleeveless dress and toe-less slippers; *they* are bandaged from head to foot in yards—nay, bolts of black serge. (And I know all about those petticoats, too. I might as well confess right here that I have one of these nuns for an aunt.) What gives? If nuns have discovered some secret form of insulation, they should share it with us sweating laymen.

Despite these smoldering resentments, I will testify—in the interests of anthropology—that the fortitude of nuns under the drill is of the highest caliber. I haven't heard a single shriek. *I'm* the only one that makes any racket but, then, the dentist is probably gentler with nuns. One little guinea pig, dead or alive, makes no difference but religious vocations are hard come by.

Could I please just talk about my dentist for a minute? This would not only give me keen pleasure (of the eye-for-an-eye, tooth-for-a-tooth variety) but, after all, she's almost next door to a nun. And, I know for certain *she's* not human.

I had thought, originally, that a Dominican Tertiary would surely approach my sensitive molars in a fine spirit of Faith, Hope and Charity. Ho! I'm now shopping around for a full-fledged pagan Witch Doctor. How that Dominican can put down the Little Office of the Virgin Mary and pick up her torture instruments with such relish is beyond me. True, she's a skillful craftsman but the Faith-Hope-Charity is at low ebb. As she drills me, she also drills home little Christian homilies.

She will say, with a non-Dominican leer: "Now *this'll* give you a rough idea of Purgatory," and down comes the needle on a quivering nerve. If I evince anything but pure delight at this golden opportunity to offer it up, she says scathingly: "It's all in your mind. *Be like the nuns.* If you would just meditate on the Joyful Mysteries as I work, you wouldn't even notice this."

If nuns can meditate in a dentist's chair, I say they are not human. (And I don't care *how* human and appealing Ingrid

Bergman was as a nun giving boxing lessons. Anyone can box. I refuse to let Hollywood sway me.)

Aside from my dental encounters with nuns, I have also met them in the nearby St. Mary's College Infirmary. Here is more fortitude but fortitude that is touching, not the kind that slays me. These are elderly nuns at the end of the trail, with their boxing days behind them. Their obediences tell the story. One year it's "Fold handkerchiefs twice a week in the laundry"; the next year it's just "Pray for the community."

But along with praying for the community, they also like to play detective. These frail and holy creatures (who wouldn't swat a fly) enjoy murder mysteries, and the more corpses strewn around the merrier. I have, rather dubiously, taken out reams of blood-curdling books to them but I guess it's all right. The Mother Superior still seems healthy enough. No one, to date, has slipped arsenic into her morning orange juice or hidden a boa constrictor under her bed. These mystery stories, in other words, do *not* counteract or supplement their reading of *The Imitation of Christ*.

One Sunday I will greet some youngster of eighty-five, rocking away and reading in a corner of the sun porch, and the next Sunday the corner is empty. The youngster is laid out in the parlor. (Death can sneak up even in the middle of an unfinished Ellery Queen.) Pinned to the mended black cape is a slip of paper showing—in neat flowing script—her original vows.

I admit I find this here-you-are, now-you-aren't situation very disconcerting, but the nuns don't. They have, as it were, their satchels all packed for the trip and are merely looking forward—cheerfully, patiently—to going home. Just around the corner is the community cemetery: row upon row of plain white crosses with—for example—"Kathleen O'Halligan" on one side and "Sister Mary Rose" on the other. Only at the end do they seem to reclaim their original identity.

This is the joker. Nuns reads detective stories but it's their own we-must-die-to-self lives that have the real mystery: concealed bodies, hidden violence, and everything. "Sister Mary Rose" must have had a death struggle with "Kathleen O'Halligan" but no X marks the scene of the crime. All that shows, on top, are the folded hands, the serene brow, the guess-what's-behind-my-smile. They make it tough going for a detective and yet, every once in a while, they get caught. They even get canonized.

The Little Flower, in her crannied wall, came the closest to getting away with the perfect crime, but when she was caught —what an exposure! It shook and affected and charmed the whole world. Yet, even in her story, you have to dig deep for clues. An amateur sleuth might be thrown off the scent by her childish watercolors, the innocent merriment of the "play hour," the scruples over enjoying a whiff of perfumed toilet water. Dig deeper and you will find a depth of strength and suffering that makes the "little way" seem the irony of ironies. What, for example, is so "little" about having to live with a lot of other women? Just one week in a Y.W.C.A. would kill *me* off.

It is for this very reason that I didn't go out of my way to collect any whimsical little human interest anecdotes about nuns. (I could quickly have had a bulging briefcase. Nuns are a happy crowd.) These are red herrings strewn across the path and I'm too smart an anthropologist to get side-tracked. These Mona Lisas are out to fool you. Let someone else, if they like, write about their humanity. I—via the dentist's chair, the infirmary, the cemetery—have given you the real low-down. Nuns are *super*human.

Consider the facts. Priests have the sacrament of Holy Orders; I have the sacrament of Matrimony; nuns have no sacrament all to themselves. Yet statistics show that there are more female saints than male saints, with nuns leading the field. How do they operate? Free wheeling?

Oh, I know *why* women take the veil (s-sh, they fell in love with a Man) but the course of true love is a bumpy one. How do they ride the bumps?

I give up. Take it away, you people who think nuns are so simple, so transparent, so easy to write about. All *I* know is that the current slogan for the *Ladies Home Journal* (Never Underestimate the Power of a Woman) must apply to many a Mona Lisa.

A Little Peach in the
Orchard Grew

ALL I had to do, said the magazine quiz, was to answer the questions truthfully and spontaneously, add up my score, and turn to page 105. On page 105 would be the grand unveiling: was I the Mother Type or was I the Wife Type?

To me, this seemed to offer a very narrow range of possibilities. What if, under my housewifely exterior, I was really the Harem Type or the Gun Moll Type or the Helen of Troy Type? None of these was very likely but, still, I resented the stuffy limitations set by this Dr. Albert O'Whoosis who had concocted the quiz. Dr. Albert O'Whoosis, not realizing that I had once been hailed as the Peach Type, was underestimating my more lush possibilities.

Back in South Bend Central High School, in the school *Interlude*, they had printed "A little peach in the orchard grew" under my graduation picture and *this*, I would have you know, was a triumph of no mean scope. Lots of the other girls had to be content with noncommittal and lacklustre sentiments like "Who shall find a valiant woman?" or "Prithee! Hark! A maid doth enter" or "Her voice was ever gentle, soft, and low, an excellent thing in woman."

At the age of seventeen, none of us gave a hoot about being soft-spoken or valiant women but "peach". . . well, now, *there* you had something. Something more on the Clara Bow order. I distinctly remember that none of the more laudable honors that came my way (making the varsity volley-ball team and winning a debate about the Panama Canal) carried the full fruity flavor of my *Interlude* analysis. Even today, whenever I open a tin of canned peaches, I always read the label (Grade A . . . hand-picked . . . packed in regulation heavy syrup) with a certain proud nostalgia. Yes, sir!

You can readily understand, therefore, why the proposed stakes in this magazine quiz hurt my feelings. Why, this up-start of a professor wasn't even giving me a *chance* to see if I had the makings of anything interesting. Just wife type or mother type, he said. MOREOVER, even meeting him on his own niggardly terms, where did he get this either/or stuff? What, pray, was to prevent me from being a perfectly peachy blend of *both*? Who, pray, was to say that Miss Peach of 1927 couldn't jolly well be Mrs. Peach of 1949?

Not Dr. O'Whoosis, by a long shot. I guessed I could show him a thing or two with one arm tied behind me. *I'd* pile up a score that would make him sit up and whistle.

The questions were awful easy. It was no strain at all to be truthful and spontaneous. The professor asked silly, easy things like: "If you had an extra five dollars, what would you buy? A new hat for yourself or one for your child?" With only a faint sneer as to what kind of a hat I'd find for five bucks nowadays, I passed on to the next one: "Would you rather curl up with a good novel or read Mother Goose aloud to the baby?" I settled that one in record time and sailed into the next bit of soul-searching: "Are you able (was I able!!) to enjoy an evening out with your husband or do you fret about the children at home?" And the question about whether or not my husband ever had to get his own breakfast made me laugh out loud. Naturally, my husband got his own break-fast. You don't expect a grown man to go to work on an empty stomach, do you?

Well, as I say, the questions were a pipe. So was my score. I barely made the grade as a wife and I failed—utterly, dis-mally—as a mother. Which just goes to show that being analyzed as a peach doesn't guarantee a blamed thing. I think the only reason I skinned through as a wife was because I

said I could enjoy a carefree evening out with my husband.
This, of course, scored heavily against me as a mother but . . .
oh, well, some days you can't make a nickel. But, even allow-
ing for the law of averages, there was no excuse for *anyone*
(outside of Dracula or Frankenstein) to flunk motherhood
with a score like mine.

"Your score of .oo8 reveals," announced Dr. O'Whoosis,
like the crack of doom, on page 105, "that you have no Mother
Instinct."

This was a fine how-do-you-do. They let you go ahead and
bear three children and *then* tell you you're not the type. Offhand, I didn't know whether I was supposed to go out and
quietly slit my own throat or else drown the three children in
the bathtub. Clearly, someone had to get out of the way.

As I tossed on my sleepless cot that night, I tried to cheer
myself up by thinking that, at any rate, my children had an
honest mother. I could have, you know, said I was crazy
about reading Mother Goose aloud and no one would have
been the wiser. And that hypothetical five bucks I spent on a
hat for myself . . . well, gee, maybe I shouldn't have done it
but I honestly thought Susie's red felt would get through
another winter. Mine was a sight.

I also made medical excuses for myself. I decided, somewhat bitterly, that the Mother Instinct was probably lacking
because my three children had all been Caesarian births.
There was probably something about having labor pains that
turned the trick. Just three days of gas pains didn't count.

With the dawn, though, I began to feel better about Mother
Goose and the hat and the gas pains. The situation was still
tense but, at least, it explained a lot of my old funny attitudes.
It explained, for example, why I have always wanted to snarl
and bite at baby photographers. Small wonder. No Mother
Instinct to make me joyously respond to their gurgling drivel.
("What a beautiful, beautiful child you have there, Mother.
Gitchee-goo, baby, gitchee-goo, Mother. By the way, you'll
want at least three gross of these oil-tinted miniatures, won't
you, Mother?")

I always thought (somewhat abashed) that I wanted to bite

photographers because I had a deficiency of calcium or some-thing in my system. I once read about a woman on a low-cal-cium diet who had an irresistible urge to bite the shoulder of a certain laundry man. The doctor advised her husband to talk the laundry man into letting her do it. Bad thing, repressions.

Now I saw no particular good reason as to why I, with no Mother Instinct to hold me back, couldn't let loose and sink my teeth into the very next photographer who gurgled at me. Come to think about it, there were lots of other people I wouldn't mind biting, either. Such as all electrical guitar, tap-dancing, baton twirling, and elocution teachers who want to groom my children for MGM, Carnegie Hall, or the Palla-dium.

Of course, these talent scouts don't start heckling you until the baby is around a year old (I understand they have minia-ture electrical guitars, infant size) but the ordinary commer-cial salesmen are on hand from birth on. Yes, I think that . . . after the photographers and talent scouts . . . I will most enjoy biting salesmen. (Naturally, I intend—thanks to Dr. O'Whoo-sis—to be an emancipated woman from now on. No more of this secret life of Walter Mitty stuff, just *dreaming* about biting.)

I'm sharpening my fangs for those salesmen who—if you resist their product—make you feel like a monster that eats its young. "You mean," they sneer, "that you intend to go through life without having your child's first shoes immortal-ized as bronze bookends? You mean you're going to make your baby eat out of a spoon that doesn't have the same design as your own Community Plate? Ugh."

Ah, how it all comes back to me. Everyone told me that my third baby would be Pure Joy ("You won't worry, you'll just enjoy him," they said) but they weren't reckoning on the commercial snakes in my Eden.

I distinctly remember the day I left the maternity ward, two years ago. With my bundle of Pure Joy in my arms, I sat there in a wheelchair waiting for the elevator. Homeward bound. My husband stood beside me, loaded with two pots of hydrangeas, a baby blanket, and my suitcase. Suddenly, a nurse raced frantically down the hall.

"Oh," she exclaimed loudly, so everyone could hear, "don't you want baby's little identification bracelet as a souvenir?" Thanking her for her thoughtfulness, I awkwardly shifted the baby and pocketed a two-inch bead bracelet that spelled out "H-a-s-l-e-y." Then, to my horror, I heard her say briskly, "And that'll be one dollar, please."

So, my husband put down the two pots of hydrangeas, the baby blanket, and the suitcase, and dragged out his wallet. It wasn't so much that it left us with just two bus tokens to get home on, understand, but the principle of the thing. With a hospital bill that would choke a horse, couldn't they have tossed that five cent bracelet in for free? A little nosegay to my motherhood? No.

One week home from the hospital, the insurance salesman showed up. Like all loving and far-sighted mothers, I wanted . . . didn't I . . . to prepare for baby's college education? I did, but I also thought it would be sort of nice if we first paid for the baby himself. I'd never forgive myself if the Finance Company came and took Danny away as they did my ironer.

By the time the Elite Studio called, my disposition was getting a little frayed around the edges.

"Is this Mrs. Louis Hasley?" the voice caroled brightly. *"Congratulations!* You have just won a contest! Your name has been selected to receive an 8 × 10 tinted picture of your new baby! When would like your appointment?"

For a split second, I thought Motherhood was going to pay off. I thought I was really going to get something for nothing, but then the bright voice caroled that—whereas the picture was free—obviously there would be a charge for the solid gold frame that went with it. Oh, obviously.

I had about lost my faith in human nature when the Welcome Wagon rolled up to my front curbing. The Welcome Wagon Lady had a market basket full of FREE gifts (all right, *be* crude and call them advertising samples) for me and my babe, all donated by local business men. This touched me to the quick. Just think! Those busy, busy tycoons taking the time to select gifts personally for poor little me. With tears smarting my eyes, I started to relieve the woman of her basket but she wouldn't let go.

It seemed that there was a little ceremony that went with the presentation and I, crude oaf that I was, was rushing the deal. Each little gift, I learned the hard way, was to be slowly and impressively lifted out—accompanied by a salestalk. My part in the ritual (and believe me, all we lacked was some background organ music) was to utter a little cluck of joy and gratitude when she finally handed it over.

I also had to remember directions. For instance, as I received a quart of homogenized milk I was told that the milkman would be around the next morning to collect the empty bottle. He was also very anxious to see how I enjoyed the way the fatty particles were all broken down and how I appreciated the 400 U. S. P. vitamin D units from irradiated ergosterol. Would I have my report ready, please, when he came? (About 6:45 A. M.)

Well, it was a bit of a nuisance to swill down the whole quart of milk that evening and prepare my testimonial but . . . there, there, I'm talking like an ingrate. The gifts *were* free and the entire ceremony only took about one and a half hours. I *was* grateful but I decided, just the same, to ask my husband to build a moat around the house to discourage further callers. The after-care of new mothers (I read somewhere) included rest and freedom from anxiety and pressing decisions.

He didn't get the moat built in time, though, to ward off Miss Pinkle, the Super Marvel Book Salesman. Miss Hattie Pinkle, a retired school teacher, caught me with my guard down because I'd caught a bad head cold (lack of rest) and didn't want to stand in the open door.

Unwittingly, I invited her to step inside but as soon as I discovered her mission in life, I began to sneeze and hack— in careless fashion—into my Kleenex. I even mentioned that tuberculosis ran rampant on my mother's side of the family but Miss Pinkle, as I learned to my sorrow, was made of stern stuff. She not only settled down on the davenport but bade me cuddle close to her so that we could look at the Super Marvel Book pictures together.

And beautiful pictures they were, too. Not to mention the valuable and illuminating printed material that went along with them. Did I know what caused lightning? Did I know the different kinds of cloud formation? Could I explain radio-activity? Did I know what makes moss grow on the north side of trees? Could I even explain the rainbow?

No. How then, asked Miss Pinkle (closing in for the kill), was I going to explain it all to my wee one when he asked me?

How, indeed? Wee one's father wasn't any help as Nature Boy; *he* just specialized in Victorian poetry at Notre Dame. But, sitting there bleary-eyed and with a tub of diapers await-ing me in the basement, I couldn't quite get into the spirit of the thing. If I furnished my wee one with dry pants, wasn't that enough? Did he have to complicate things by asking about lightning? But I knew, deep down inside of me, that I was being an unimaginative dolt about the whole affair. Mak-ing rapid calculations, I figured that we could (by just living on rice) probably finish paying the last installments on the book by 1964.

Then a horrible thought struck me. If my wee one never asked what made lightning (and *I* wasn't going to bring it up) why . . . why, it would just mean our life savings down the sink. Not to mention getting beriberi from the steady rice diet.

Wouldn't it be far more sensible never to let my wee one see lightning? Lock him in a closet every time it stormed? Or (and this was more constructive), why not give wee one a piece of string and a key and push him out in the storm to discover and harness lightning for himself? After all, no one made things easy for Benjamin Franklin.

So I said, out loud: "No one made it easy for B. Frank-lin."

Miss Pinkle looked so dazed that, warming to my theme, I launched into the rugged boyhood of Franklin, the Wright Brothers, Robert Fulton, Marconi and Edison. Did they have the Super Marvel Books? Not on your life. Triumphantly, I pointed out that to have such books within easy reach would soften a lad's moral fibre, quench the spark for research, stunt his ingenuity, dull his boyish curiosity at God's natural wonders. . . .

Well, I put in a hard morning's work but Miss Pinkle finally slunk out the front door: dazed, converted, apologetic. The last I heard of her she had given up her shady traffic in worthwhile books and was selling ladies' ready-to-wear in Penny's basement. So I guess I outwitted Miss Pinkle, all right, but look at the time and the energy I had to expend in order to save face. If I had only known *then* what I know *now* —to wit, no Mother Instinct, like an albatross around my neck—I could just have laughed in Miss Pinkle's face.

"Ha," I could have laughed in Miss Pinkle's face, "so you think I'm interested in my own children, eh? Make tracks, Pinkle."

Well, you can see for yourself just how indebted I am to Dr. Albert O'Whoosis for this new freedom. (You can also see for yourself just what the years have done to the little peach in the orchard growing but let's skip lightly over that, shall we?) Actually, I can hardly wait for him to bring out another quiz and let me find out some more about myself.

Here We Go Round the Mulberry Bush

ONCE upon a time, at a Catholic Action Rally, all the delegates were asked to stand up, give their names, and tell what group they represented. So, solemnly, delegate after delegate arose and spoke his little piece.

"I'm from Friendship House," one girl said. "I represent the magazine INTEGRITY," said another. "I'm from Monica House" . . . "I belong to the Young Christian Workers" . . . "I represent the Grail" . . . "I'm a Christopher" . . . "I'm with the Christ Child movement" . . . "I'm with the Catholic Worker" . . . "I belong to the Convert Makers of America" . . . "I'm with . . ."

Down the impressive list they went until they got to one girl who was sitting rather quietly on the sidelines. "And you . . . ?" asked the chairman.

The girl got up, visibly embarrassed. "Gee, I guess I don't belong here," she said. "I'm just a Catholic."

This little story (lifted, unscrupulously, from the *Catholic Interracialist*) delighted my soul, because my soul, of late, has been rather perturbed. Like that girl, I—too—sit more or less on the sidelines: following the big league players with the aid of a scoreboard, applauding vigorously at all home runs, and cheering for my own special favorites. But it isn't my role as spectator that bothers me. Not at all. What bothers me is that I, in the grandstand, don't like to see my players go too professional.

When these apostles get to the point when they think that *only* the C.M.O.A. or the C.Y.O. or the Y.C.W. or the N.C.C.W. or what-initials-have-you is the approved way to restore all things in Christ, then they need some apostolic attention themselves. *Or* (same tune, different lyrics): "Who takes care of the caretaker's daughter while the caretaker's busy taking care?"

Maybe they need a brief spell of sitting on the benches . . . cooling off, thinking things over . . . before barging onto the field again.

From where I'm sitting (and, I admit, it's easy to be mellow and tolerant when you're just sitting), it looks as if these apostles often go beyond the "Aw, this arguing is just good, clean, Catholic fun" stage. When you start drawing blood, it seems to me, the merriment is o'er. And whereas the participants can perhaps bind up their own wounds and prevent gangrene from setting in, what about the innocent bystander who listens in on the fracas?

His illusions can plop to the sidewalk like the pods from a shedding catalpa tree. Far better to sit safely at home and twiddle your thumbs, he reasons, than join up with the "wrong" sorority. To be a fool for Christ sounds good but to risk being just a plain danged fool is something else again. But gee, he'd heard that the Pope himself was strongly urging this lay apostolate business and it all sounded so heroic and so inspiring and now . . . well, gee. . . .

"The most compelling ideal," says Ed Willock in *Ye Gods*, "can become like a foolish dream once it encounters the vicious tongue of the wisecracker. Like the subway artist, the gag man can always crayon a mustache or an absurd pair of spectacles on his own or another man's vision of greatness."

Yet to propose the obvious . . . c'est à dire, the crying need for more charity among the brethren . . . is to invite the heavens to fall upon you.

"Charity is fine," the apostles cry in unison, "but *compromise* is a different kettle of fish. In the Christian life there can be no compromise; the road is straight and narrow. Naturally, we *all* want to restore all things in Christ but my benighted confrères over there are beating the empty air, if not actually damaging the Cause."

Individually, these apostolic souls (who don't always, alack, *accurately* represent their various groups) lift their confused voices like unto this:

"One thing is certain," states an *Integrity* editor, as if issuing a Papal Bull. "Being is more important than doing. You can't radiate Christ until Christ is within you. You can't give what you haven't got."

"Wait a minute, pal," says a Father Keller disciple. "I know just who you're looking at. So all right, being *is* more important than doing but where do you draw the line? How do you gauge a guy's personal holiness? Got a thermometer? Frankly, I think *your* outfit is spiritually snobbish. To hear you blast off, one might think that only the daily communicants have an inside track with God and that the good will of a 'beginner' isn't worth a fig newton. But if we all wait until we're ready to be canonized before lifting a finger, nothing will be accomplished. No, sir, *any* Christian can be an apostle in some small way. 'Better to light one candle than . . .' "

"I know, I know," interrupts an impatient liturgist. "Write it to your Congressman, Christopher, but spare *me*, please. Personally, I put more stock in the Early Fathers than that Dale Carnegie stuff. Yes, the only solution is to go back to the Early Fathers . . . drink at the pure sources. . . ."

"Tosh," says a Jocist admirer. "How do the Early Fathers know what's needed for 1949? The Pope himself has told us to develop bold and daring techniques to suit the times. Why, look at those priests working in the factories in France! They're not urging the downtrodden mill hands to say Compline; they're first trying to win them over to Christianity, not just Catholicism, by being their brother's keeper. A living wage . . . three meals a day . . . a decent roof over their heads. First things first, chum. Yes, what Catholics need today is to forget their own precious soul-polishing for a minute and practice plain natural charity. That's the universal language. Anyone can understand charity."

"Come, come," says the apologist. "Aren't you putting that charity on a purely material basis? The Communists can do as much. Soup is soup but Truth is Truth. Man doth not live by bread alone and Truth is the answer to today's problems."

"No, no," cries a N.C.C.W. delegate. "I know *your* outfit. You'd shove a pamphlet down a man's throat even if he was starving to death. Or if he couldn't even read. One can always spot the people *you're* trying to help by the hunted look in their eyes. Besides, *your* idea of Truth is to be able to talk back to Maritain while I belong to the school of 'I'd rather feel compunction than know how to define it.' Our own private lives and examples (especially us women!) are a more powerful influence than free soup, liturgy, apologetics, or marching in picket lines."

"But," says a Y.C.W. girl, "your private life, spotless though it be, can be a light under the bushel. Frankly, I don't see how you can tell a good Catholic from a good Presbyterian, twenty yards off. It's the Catholic's job to stand out as something *more* than an upright and moral citizen."

"As for me," murmurs a Third Order postulant piously, "I only came to this noisy rally in order to announce our new class in Gregorian singing but, aside from that, I wash my hands of *all* this bustle and activity. I will sit in my corner, praising God through my breviary, and let the Holy Ghost do my work in the world."

"But," answers the Y.C.W. gal, "faith without works is dead. You're still very much in the world, friend, and perfectly able-bodied, aren't you? Moreover, your Holy Ghost doesn't operate just like incense. The Holy Ghost works through people . . . and books . . . and chance encounters . . ."

"You're all barking up the wrong tree," announces *Integrity*. "Guess you didn't read our last issue where we explained that we can't change people until we change their vicious surroundings. As any fool can plainly see, industrialism is the root of all evil. We must return to the ways of the Middle Ages and bring back the craftsmen and, with them, man's self-respect and integrity and creative impulses. This de-humanization is simply . . ."

"That's true," interrupts the Grail. "Why, if women would only start grinding their own whole wheat flour and making their own cottage cheese instead of . . ."

"Fiddle-dee-dee," objects another. "Your Grail and its cottage cheese is all right for preparing girls for rural life but it's a big laugh in the city. So is all that return to the Middle Ages stuff. No, we must take the world as it is, not tilt at windmills. The movies, radio, video, etc., are good in themselves but they're being perverted. We must turn them into true and positive channels of communication. We must go into the marketplace and get key positions and influence the tycoons . . ."

"Look, Christopher," cries a student contributor to *Concord*, "don't you mean just to hop on the gravy boat along *with* those tycoons? Perhaps get your little kernel of truth mixed with all the pap now and then and perhaps jeopardize your own soul in the process? Besides, aren't you forgetting that it's too late in the day to educate the adults in the market-place? The hope of the Church lies in its *youth*. We must train our Catholic Action college students to apply Catholicism to current problems and then go forth and . . ."

"College?" screams the editor of *Today*. "Too late! Too late! It's the teen-age group that's in the plastic stage."

"Teen-age?" snorts a loyal Father Peyton follower. "Too late! Too late! We must start teaching youth in the cradle, at mother's knee. Now the Family Rosary Crusade tries . . ."

"Yes," pipes up a Christ Child member timidly, "but doesn't the baby need diapers before a rosary? Our group, in making layettes, encourages . . ."

"Hold everything!" pleads a Cana Conference organizer. "Before furnishing diapers, let's worry about furnishing the babies themselves. Actually, everything . . . and I *do* mean everything . . . depends on the integrity of the family unit. Now in our Family Movement group we sponsor . . ."

"Maybe," says another prayerfully, "we better just leave the born Catholics out of this. Now the C.M.O.A. is out to make converts . . . they're the ones that bring in the new fresh blood and we can't leave *all* the work to Fulton Sheen . . . and let the lukewarm and fallen-aways alone. Let's win new souls for Christ and let the Catholic weaklings shift for themselves."

The Legion of Mary bristles: "Not bring back God's lost ones? Not seek out the black sheep in our hospitals and jails and flop houses? Why, there is more rejoicing in Heaven o'er . . ."

"You mean well, sister," says *Integrity* kindly, "and our hearts *do* bleed for your sheep, but I guess you didn't read our issue on the new apostolate. To repeat, time is running short. A new world is being formed (by the way, didn't you even read Cardinal Suhard's pastoral letter? Tsk.) and we can't let it form without us. Ergo, we must raise up an elect band, the new leaven in the loaf; concentrate on quality rather than quantity. Unfortunately, we have only two hands and so we must be ruthless in not wasting time on the chicken feed."

"But," says the Legion in tears, "that's as bad as euthanasia. What's Stalin got that you haven't got?"

"She's right," says Friendship House staunchly. "The Mystical Body draws no lines. I am the Vine, you are the branches. Who is to say one soul is more precious than another? It all goes together, it all goes together . . . this binding up Christ's wounds. But if you ask *me* . . . well, our group, fighting for racial justice, is cauterizing mankind's worst sore."

"That's a good sideline," admits another, "but look here, folks. Aren't we ignoring our most obvious answer? Our group, in promoting devotion to our Lady of Fatima, puts all these problems in Our Lady's lap. The Rosary is the weapon of the twentieth century and so let us become as little children and do our Lady's simple bidding . . ."

"Fine, fine," says a Catholic Worker wearily, "but Our Lady doesn't say to grab up a rosary and tell the soup lines to scram. And isn't an act of charity in His name an 'Ave' in itself? More, we must be truly astonishing in our charity *and* our penance, for one must not underestimate the apostolate of suffering. We must not help people across polished desks but go down to their level to reach out to them . . . live as they do, suffer as they do. And Lady Poverty is a sweet mistress who will . . ."

"*That* part is all right," says another coolly, "and you probably have real saints in your outfit. But what about that dizzy pacifist angle you push? Of all the cock-eyed, un-American . . ."

And thus it goes, round and round the mulberry bush, until one is tempted to yell: "*Is* there a theologian in the house who can settle all this yakity-yak? Only a theologian, with a three-foot beard and a dozen degrees, can possibly serve as an adequate referee."

Or is it just possible, say I timidly (for my beard and degrees are conspicuous by their absence) that the answer is very old and simple? Namely, the imitation of Christ.

Christ's first apostles were certainly a motley crew of the washed and the unwashed and, in 1949 A.D., it's still the same old story. Yet if Christ could put up with them with good grace, why can't we? Moreover, Christ must have had a good reason for selecting all sorts of types to reach out to all sorts of other types. The blatant, the subtle; the brash, the timid; the dreamers, the realists; the glamorous, the plodders . . .

Perhaps Christ even knew what He was doing when He *didn't* draw up a practical handbook, with footnotes and diagrams, on "Rules and Regulations for the Lay Apostolate." Instead, He just kept saying: "I am the Way." Not: "There is only one way to draw others to the One Way."

Personally, I can just see those early apostles fitting right into their twentieth century grooves. Martha washing up the dishes in Friendship House kitchen while Sister Mary chats with Bishop Sheil in the library. Paul preaching from a soapbox in Times Square. Lazarus giving new life to the dead souls in a Catholic Worker flophouse. The "woman at the well," with her so-called five husbands, becoming a Christopher in her Beverly Hills neighborhood. Nicodemus running a Catholic Information Center. Young Stephen promoting a C.Y.O. Conference. Impatient Peter working on the staff at *Integrity*. I can even imagine Peter exclaiming, as at Thabor: "It is good, Lord, to be here. Let us start three *more* Catholic magazines. . . ."

And, as before, we would find Mary, the Mother of God, making a home for John and "just being a Catholic."

Let the congregation arise and sing hymn number 82—in unison, if possible—and leave to God the awarding of the individual halos.

My Public, Right or Wrong

I HAVE long toyed with the idea of getting this out of my system. I think I'd feel better, much better, if I could just get into cold print what I think of my ever-responsive public. Goodness knows that *they're* having a good time telling what they think of me.

That's the rub. Everyone wants to get into the act. I may not have much of a reading public but what there is of it is most certainly a writing public. Nearly everything I produce (and it's not everyone that has my talent for bringing out the beast in people) prompts my readers to leap to their type-writers. Naturally these goaded souls have to find some sort of release but if they would *just* use discretion. That's all I ask, discretion.

If these knife-in-the-back letters would just land in my own mailbox, all would be well. I have plenty of wastebaskets around and, aside from my own bleeding back, no one would be the wiser. But they don't! Thoughtless citizens send their disgruntled complaints smack to the editor, thus playing havoc with this tender budding career of mine. I daresay this is the general idea, but *I* say live and let live.

I divide these writers into two classes: the ones that like me (the sensitive and discriminating type, obviously) and the non-discriminating dullards who would just as lief I were dead. For some peculiar reason, it's the dullards who are in the majority and so it's the dullards I must take firmly in hand. My career, precarious at best, demands it.

Heaven only knows how many "Cancel-my-subscription-*immediately*" letters I have brought down on the heads of editors brash enough to print my stuff. I'm afraid to ask. Offhand, I imagine I could—if given a fighting chance—pull a magazine's circulation down lower than France's birth rate. I simply can't understand this. Here I am, sweating like a mule driver, trying to be funny; trying my best to cheer a downtrodden world with cute whimsical essays.

What do I receive (aside from the check) in return? Plaintive requests to give my typewriter to the Salvation Army, take a slow boat to China, break my right arm, or—better still—go join the Foreign Legion Auxiliary. Can't understand it.

My husband, though, thinks that crime does not pay, that I get what's coming to me. *He* thinks my sparkling wit and humor is the equivalent to a hearty slap on the back before breakfast. *He* thinks my humor is definitely perverted.

So what if I do exaggerate a wee bit? Can I help it if I'm the type that never says "I'm warm" but "I roast, I swelter, I broil . . . I am like to die?" All I'm really saying is that I'm sorta warmish and would like to gripe a little about the weather. It does *not* mean that I expect my readers immediately to raise funds to send me on a North Pole expedition. So why can't people just whittle my statements down to life size and then swallow them along with a box of Morton's free-running iodized salt? It would certainly be much easier than for me, at this late date, to reform.

It comforts me to know that Mark Twain had the same vice. When a neighbor asked his mother, "Do you ever believe anything that that boy tells you?" his mother replied, "He is the wellspring of truth, but you can't bring up the whole well in one bucket. I know his average, therefore he never deceives me. I discount him 90% for embroidery, and what is left is perfect and priceless truth, without a flaw in it anywhere." A boy's best friend is his mother.

However, back to my own defense. The whole trouble, as I see it, is that people do not read my essays *carefully* enough. In everything I write there is hidden at least one morsel of

Pure Truth but people just don't seem to have the patience to dig around for it. They give up too easily; they haven't got that good old pioneering spirit.

Let me illustrate. I recently wrote an essay entitled "How To Make A Convert Singlehanded": a very helpful contribution to the propagation of the Faith. True, I'd never made a convert in my life but I had some very fancy theories as to how, with a little cunning, it might possibly be arranged. Moreover, in my very first paragraph—right in plain sight —was my little nugget of Pure Truth. To wit, I graciously allowed as how God had quite a bit to do with convert-making.

Did anyone read my first paragraph? Guess not. Missionaries from all over the place—from swamps, jungles, bayous, and desert plains—immediately rushed to God's defense and my confusion. And that, my friends, is the way my edifying articles seem to hit people. With one accord, they all turn around and try to convert me all over again. The original idea, you understand, was that *I* was to do the edifying (not bring out the missionary spirit, full blast, in others) but that isn't the way it's turning out. The way it's turning out, I have more people trying to save my soul than you can shake a stick at. Naturally, I don't mind being prayed over but it hurts my feelings that they think I need so *many* prayers.

To continue with my own defense (and it's about time *someone* stepped in), I seem to fare no better in the realm of pure humor. When I write something riotously funny, I want it clearly understood that people are supposed to *laugh*. If this is patently impossible (even God does not demand the impossible), then why don't people—since they were foolhardy enough to read it in the first place—just be good sports? From a practical standpoint, there are *no refunds*, so why don't they just offer it up for the Poor Souls? *Why*, for Pete's sake, must they take *this* poor soul so seriously?

Let me again illustrate. (And, so help me, this is perfect and flawless truth.) I once wrote a light and harmless essay entitled *Janet Takes Piano Lessons*. You wouldn't think that would get me into trouble, would you? Listen.

Janet is my daughter who has not an ounce of music in her
young bones. Well, first thing I knew I had mortally wounded
piano lovers from coast to coast. No one cared how much *I*
suffered from Janet's rendition of "The Pow-Wow Dance"
but they were dreadfully concerned about the inhuman treatment meted out to the *piano.* All I said was that the piano
was a beast of burden, with the top loaded with hats, comic
books, yo-yos, dry cleaner's stubs, prayer books, and money
for the paper boy. That I found mittens and half-eaten cookies
between the sheet music; the dextrose from gnawed Tootsie
Rolls all over the keys.

I also added that I could—working diligently, and with no
phone interruptions—clean it all up in an hour's time. Yet
no one noted *that* housewifely touch. What I got was this,
printed in the Letters to the Editor Department, from a Detroit music teacher:

"As a piano teacher experienced in modern methods of
imparting a working knowledge of that instrument to the
younger generation, I resent Mrs. Hasley's attitude. Mani-
festly, Mrs. Hasley does not feel a proper respect for the piano
either as a musical instrument or piece of furniture. I wonder
if gnawed Tootsie Rolls ornament other articles of furniture
in the Hasley home," etcetera, etcetera.

This made me plenty sore. Not only was it *my* piano (I
could pour molasses over it if I felt in the mood), but why
should that Detroit music teacher go snooping through the
rest of my house? I was tempted to write back, savagely:
"Right. I live in a hovel. I am a natural born slattern. If you
think my piano is a mess, you should peek in my dresser
drawers . . ."

Before I got this nasty rebuttal off, unknown friends (sensitive, discriminating) rose to my defense, and so I put away
my shotgun. But by the time they were all through batting
me around, I felt like a badminton bird after a hard session.

Then there was an article entitled "I Like Priests." Mothers
of female religious immediately demanded a re-deal. What
was the matter with me? What did I have against nuns? I'd
better make good on this or else . . .

So, I obligingly wrote a toast to the nuns and then sat back, complacently waiting for the world to thank me. My first inkling that the world was *not* thanking me was the reception of an anonymous postcard, writ in pencil, that announced: "If you was a good Catholic, you would not write like you does about the Holy Nuns." This is what is commonly known as throwing bread upon the waters and getting back a slug of arsenic.

Perhaps the worst letters (still steadily burning a hole in my files) followed an essay entitled *Reproachfully Yours,* dedicated to the priest who converted me. All I said was that he left an awful lot out of my instructions; that he left me ill-fortified to run the whole gauntlet of liturgical ritual by myself. I proceeded to cite, with relish, my woes as I faced the Holy Roman Catholic Church after twenty-one years as a peaceful law-abiding Presbyterian. As I wrote it, *I* thought it so funny that I could scarce control myself.

So?

(A.) There was a phone call from the local Epworth League, delicately hinting that I did not seem quite, *quite* happy with my new religion. Anytime I wanted to switch back . . . well, I could always count on the good old Epworth League. After an agonized, sweating explanation that I *liked* being a Catholic, the Epworth Leaguer broke into uncouth laughter. It was just one of my new Catholic friends, holding his nose to disguise his voice. Just good clean Catholic fun, see?

(B.) An anonymous donor (distressed because I complained of getting tangled up in the ribbons of my missal) sent me a year's subscription to the Leaflet Missal. No ribbons. Even a baby could manage it.

(C.) A Canadian truck driver sent me a seven page letter, typed on both sides single spaced, pouring out *his* troubled soul. I had troubles? I should listen to his'n. Moreover, my anti-clerical tendencies—said he!—assured him of a sympathetic audience. The gist of his anti-clerical tirade was that he didn't like the new carpeting in the vestibule—the priest hadn't consulted him—and that he *couldn't* make the First Fridays. On his first attempt he got trapped by a Good Friday.

On the second try, the priest went away on his vacation just as he'd worked up to Friday #8. He was pretty bitter about the whole thing. What a chase, said he, to get to Heaven.

(D.) A lady from Boston wrote the *editor* (Help! Murder!): "Let Mrs. Hasley be as St. Aloysius who always pondered 'How will my writing be judged in the light of Eternity?' "

This was pretty stiff. It reduced me—before the mailman had even rounded the corner—to a quivering scrupulous pulp. Clearly, I had not been following in the pious and prudent footsteps of Aloysius.

In alarm (I didn't *really* want to be tossed back to the Epworth League), I abandoned the Catholic essay for the tolerant field of secular fiction. I fared no better. I wrote a story called *The Sweater Girls*, wherein the man of the house (a cad, if ever) took a shine to their fifteen year old baby sitter.

You guessed it. The local citizens began to pat my hand, heave dolorous sighs, be unduly and suspiciously kind to me. Finally the rumors hit my ears: "I guess the Hasleys aren't getting along . . . where *else* would she get her material . . . she's given him the best years of her life . . . never can tell about those quiet Notre Dame professors . . . still waters run deep, you know" . . .

Ah, well, this is the price—I reckon—for one's Art. But, like a Hollywood movie star disguising herself with dark glasses and then planting herself at a ringside table at the Brown Derby, don't think I don't enjoy my public. It's my public, right or wrong. If no one paid *any* attention to me, I'd go out and eat worms.